Health Inspector, *Eh?*

Memoir by a Health Inspector

PETER K.P. LEE,

CPHI (C)

 **FriesenPress**

Suite 300 - 990 Fort St
Victoria, BC, Canada, V8V 3K2
www.friesenpress.com

Copyright © 2015 by Peter K. P. Lee
First Edition — 2015

ISBN
978-1-4602-6055-5 (Hardcover)
978-1-4602-6056-2 (Paperback)
978-1-4602-6057-9 (eBook)

1. Biography & Autobiography, Law Enforcement

Distributed to the trade by The Ingram Book Company

Table of Contents

Acknowledgements

I want to thank my wife, my daughter and my son for their constant encouragement in making this memoir. Both children provided constant and patient assistance that contributed to the completion of this book. Above all, I want to thank God for blessing me with a challenging career, an interesting life, and a wonderful family.

Background

I was born in Mainland China and I grew up in Hong Kong for most of my childhood. My father passed away when I was twelve years old, and three years later, I immigrated to Vancouver with my mother.

I attended an English school when I was in Hong Kong until Form 2 or 3, which is equivalent to Grade 8 or 9 in the British Columbia educational system. Whatever English that I had learned there didn't seem to help me when I arrived in Vancouver. I attended one month of 'New Canadian School' at the Vancouver Laura Secord School, and was then placed in Britannia Secondary School at the Grade 10 level. It was a struggle to learn English and to catch up with other classmates. I remember that for social studies class, I was told to read two or three chapters daily, but had use a dictionary to understand most of it. The only subject that gave me no problems was math. I struggled very hard for three years and I finally graduated from Britannia Secondary School in 1968.

After my high school graduation, I went to the British Columbia Institute of Technology (BCIT) for two years and completed the Biological Science Technology, Horticulture program. We were the first graduates with the horticulture option in 1970. We looked forward to employment as landscapers, landscape designers, or gardeners. After graduation from BCIT, I looked for landscaping designing jobs but had no success. I ended up working as a landscaper for a contractor later at the University of British Columbia Physical Plant Department and at the Vancouver School Board as a gardener. Because of the nature of outdoor gardening work, and being the lowest on the seniority list, I was laid off as soon as winter arrived and became unemployed for a few months.

In the summer of 1971, I went back to BCIT to take the Environmental Health, Public Health program. First, I had to meet and to consult with an admission adviser, Don, a Public Health Inspector who was working in Vancouver Health Department at that time and who warned me about discrimination in the health inspection field, especially for a person of Chinese origin. That did not discourage me, but I was glad to be fore-warned about it; it helped me to understand some extraordinary situations, particularly during my earlier career. Discrimination happened, but I did not allow myself to be belittled. I learned to simply ignore such ignorant attitudes. I was interviewed but was eventually turned down for quite a few job openings in the Vancouver Lower Mainland area while working in Redwater, Alberta. I wondered if that had anything to do with being Chinese-Canadian.

In the summer of 1973, I graduated from the Public Health program along with about forty other graduates. The majority of the graduates got job offers and I accepted a position to work in a brand new one-man sub-office in Redwater, Alberta.

Health Inspector, *Eh?*

Chapter 1

Good-Bye to my Career and Welcome to Retirement

Thursday, September 29, 2011—my last working day prior to retirement. After today, I will be on a long vacation leave the next three months and my official retirement will actually begin in the first week of February. I went to my former office in West Vancouver to say good bye to some of the nicer staff.

It was 1:30 and I was going to the last PHI/EHO staff meeting, which was supposed to end at 2:30, and would be followed by my retirement tea-party. I was very much into the meeting and even a few times offered my opinions and my observations regarding some of the challenging work issues. During the meeting, a new "Hedge-Hog" inspection form was shown and discussed. The new Personal Services Regulation and the new Pool Regulation were introduced. The enforcement action and expectation of these two new regulations were also presented by our manager. In my heart, I was glad to be retiring and that these new regulations would be left behind.

Finally, the staff meeting was wrapped up slightly over schedule and my tea-party started. Everyone was busy bringing out the final touch of their masterpiece food items. The party started slowly at first. I was surprised to see Sue, a long time Public Health Nurse who just retired two weeks before me. I felt bad that I didn't even go to her retirement banquet. Then came Masumi, the physiotherapist; Ruth, the downstairs clerk; Denny, the former PHI practicum student, and many others.

All of a sudden, I saw a tall figure walking into the room and I was shocked when I realized that the tall figure was Charlie, my former chief, whom I had not heard from or seen since he retired from BCIT quite sometime before. We reminisced and chatted about the old days. Then came Richard, the VCH Environmental Health Director, and Angelo, the VCH Environmental Health Manager.

One person who came to the party was not welcome because my career advancement was blocked by this individual, even though I still do not know why. In a way, I am glad that person came to my party because it was evident that I was well-liked inside and outside the Health Department, and deemed an excellent health inspector by my peers.

In my career, I came across several unlikable colleagues. I remember a movie with my favourite actor, Sean Connery, who quoted a Chinese old saying: "If you stay beside the river long enough, you will see the corpse of your enemy floating by." I did see several of these not very likable colleagues get what they deserved at the end.

Paul, my manager, asked me to stand beside him in front of all the staff and guests. He began to speak about my more than thirty-eight year career working as a PHI, some of my philosophies, and some of my memorable working experiences. Particularly memorable was the supervision of an exhumation in the District of North Vancouver Cemetery behind Capilano College, and also supervising the destruction of about $50,000 worth of liquor crushing by a bulldozer in the District of North Vancouver Landfill. Charlie remembered those two incidents and responded excitedly. Paul did a great job and I appreciated his efforts. The tea-party was filled with joy and lots of laughter. It was really beyond my expectations.

Thinking back, my long career went by in a flash. Of course, I had some ups and downs during this time. One thing for sure is that I very much enjoy working with the public. I found the majority of people to be law-abiding citizens that are willing to co-operate and comply with health regulations. Of course, a small percentage of people will not co-operate because they are running into financial problems, on the verge of bankruptcy, or simply hate or distrust bureaucrats. I had observed some of my past colleagues' conduct and it is no wonder some individuals do not trust the government. But in every profession there will always be, as Clint Eastwood's movie calls it, the good, the bad, and the ugly.

You would think that, given the nature of my enforcement work, my enemy or obstacle would be the public that I had to deal with every day, but it was actually the opposite. The real problem was the management and office administration. The inconsistent policies and practices often created confusion and unnecessary conflicts. I always got my job done on time and also got along very well with the majority of the public.

The Trans Fat Regulation in 2009, the new Swimming Pool Regulation of 2011, and the voluntary compliance regarding labelling of the salt and sugar content in restaurant meals are some of the main reasons for my early retirement. I personally don't agree that the government should regulate our food, like how much fat, trans fat, sugar, or salt the public should consume. I believe that public health should educate and not regulate these kinds of areas. For example, look at the regulations around smoking and tobacco sales. They are getting more and more stringent as time goes on, but belligerent or hard-headed smokers will smoke no matter what. I felt that we did the best by educating them and if some individuals continue to smoke and don't comply, this is their choice.

I personally don't agree with the direction of the Health Authority to intrude and interfere in the citizens' private lives. It is contradictory to me that the government regulates smoking, trans fat, sugar, and salt intake, yet at the same time, the government in Canada and United States are talking about legalizing the possession in small quantities and recreation usage of marijuana.

About three weeks after my retirement, shopping in the malls and supermarkets seemed normal as usual, but for the first time, I felt like I had lost my identity. For almost forty years, I always walked into a supermarket or restaurant and identified myself as a Health Inspector, but now I am no longer able to do that. However, I still feel like I am and automatically check for wrong processes or violations as soon as I walk in. Once a Health Inspector, always a Health Inspector.

I was twenty-two years old when I became a Public Health Inspector. Immediately after graduation from B.C. Institute of Technology in 1973, I was hired by the Sturgeon Health Unit in St. Albert, Alberta. I was stationed in a brand new, one-man office in Redwater, a small town with a population of a thousand about seventy kilometers northeast of St. Albert. This position was first given to one of our top students, who later declined. We had about forty students in our graduating class. Ninety percent received employment a short time after graduation, often scattered all over Canada. At the time of my retirement and to the best of my knowledge, there were only a handful of these graduates still working in the health inspection field.

I was very fortunate that I took my PHI practicum in Prince George in 1972 with a very trusting Chief Public Health Inspector, Norm. I remember that a few days after I started my field training, my Chief PHI simply gave me the BC government car key and told me to go out and inspect. During that time in Prince George, health inspectors were very involved with sewage disposal systems and new subdivisions as the top priority. During my field training, I was inspecting about ten sewage disposal systems per day. The systems were mainly septic tanks for smaller residential lots and sewage lagoons for larger 5 acre lots. I did a few rock-pits and Nodak-Mounts as well. In the later part of my field training, to catch up with the food premises inspection, the Chief PHI requested me to inspect a great number of restaurants on my own in the city of Prince George.

Soon, my three months of field training was completed at the end of August, 1972. My training was fruitful and challenging. Later, I learnt that some of my classmates were trained at other health units as observers and without much opportunity to do inspections on their own. It is not the same when you are always tagging along with another inspector. It is very different when you are inspecting on your own and when operators or the public are expecting answers or advice directly from you. Of course, you have to be self-confident and also know the limit of knowledge and authority as a PHI trainee. When I was out in the field inspecting during my practicum, I always consulted by phone with the Chief PHI or someone else in the office for advice.

I was fortunate again when I started working on my first job as a certified Public Health Inspector because I had a wonderful Senior PHI, Ken, who provided me all the support and encouragement right through my learning stage. I really respected him as a friend, a boss, and a mentor. I am very thankful that he led me to accept the Lord Jesus Christ as my personal saviour. My Christian faith really helped me through many of my difficult situations in my career and my family. I remember many times that I prayed and turned it over to God, and the difficult situation would be resolved miraculously. God is mighty and able to do wonderful things.

In this memoir I will illustrate some unusual, funny, weird, and extraordinary experiences of my Health Inspector career of 38 plus years. I will share "the good, the bad and the ugly," dealing with the public, the administration, and family life. The public and those whose lives are directly or indirectly in contact with health inspectors can gain some valuable insight into this often misunderstood, but vital profession.

Chapter 2

Public Health Inspector (PHI) in the rural area vs. Big City

As I was completing my program at BCIT, I decided to accept the first employment offer from anywhere in Canada. I was even prepared to go to work up north in the Territories. It was my intention to come back to work in the Vancouver area eventually after a few years. Because of the wonderful working relationship that I had with my Senior PHI at Redwater for two years, it was a very difficult decision for me to leave in the summer of 1975. I had learned a lot from my time there.

When I started to work in Redwater, Alberta, as a PHI, my district was about 250 square kilometers and included many small towns and hamlets. It was quite a shock for a city boy like me to go into a small hamlet that only has 3 or 4 houses and a population of twelve or so. To get between these villages, I could easily put in 250 kilometers of driving in one work day. Another thing that I was not used to was driving on the muddy or country gravel roads. On a typical water sampling day, I may only meet five or six people after driving over a hundred kilometres.

Three months after I started working in early September, the first snow came and I drove right into the highway ditch because I braked too sharply. I eventually learned how to pump the brake like a pro. One time, the brake line was broken and I lost all the fluid, but I had to keep driving. The only way that I could stop was to control my speed and estimate the stopping distance required, hoping the car would stop as I planned. I did manage to drive back safely to Redwater and drop off the car at a local garage to get the brakes repaired.

I remember one time that I got stuck in the muddy country road at a remote farm in the middle of nowhere. I put twigs and dry hay under the wheels to provide traction. I kept trying and trying. Thank God, I was eventually freed up and got back to the highway.

The prairie winter was another condition that I was not used to. During the first winter, the temperature dipped down to minus fifty Celsius, plus the wind chill factor. I had to quickly buy proper winter clothing—and shoes as well after I slipped and landed on my back several times walking on ice with my Vancouver summer shoes. I also learned to keep my car engine block-heater plugged in outside a highway coffee shop while having a coffee-break to ensure it would start when I come out.

I remember one time I was driving out from Redwater to Edmonton for an appointment, and the outside temperature was about minus forty-five degrees Celsius, with a wind chill on top. The temperature gauge in my car was staying at about a third and never reached normal, even after more than an hour of driving at highway speed. I was glad to be able to experience the cold prairie weather that words cannot describe. I kept a survival kit consisting of a blanket, a small shovel, matches, candles and chocolate bars in the trunk of the car. During the cold prairie winter, people can easily lose their lives if they get stuck in a remote farm without heat and food. I heard horror stories about drivers who got stuck in their car in the remote countryside and they would light a candle, and pull out and burn the car upholstery just to keep warm.

During Christmas time in 1974, I had a car accident coming home from St. Albert to Redwater at night, right in the middle of a blizzard. I was not injured seriously but I did bump my head on the roof of my car and it gave me a headache for about a week. The front driver's-side fender of my car was ripped out. I should have stayed overnight at my senior PHI's home. That was the first lesson for me about driving in blizzard conditions. All that I could see was the glare from the on-coming cars. I could only see a few feet in front of my windshield. I also remember that I had to shovel the entire lane behind my apartment so I could drive out. The overnight snow drift often prevented the door from opening the next morning.

It was quite an adventure for a young city boy like me. At times I felt lonely, but I have no regrets for the two years I spent in Redwater. Working as a Public Health Inspector in a rural area was quite different from working in a big metropolitan area. People in the rural areas are generally more relaxed and not in a hurry. Farmers love to talk to you and share their stories. I remember during inspection, several female restaurant operators burst into tears because of family problems with their spouses or children. The prairie people are more hospitable and friendly. My Senior PHI told me about one incident when a farmer came after him with a hunting rifle due to some disagreements. I think this is because people are not happy any time the answer is 'no'. I also had several contentious experiences by saying 'no' to the public and operators in my working life as a PHI, as I recount in the following chapter.

When I was hired back to a big city on the North Shore in the summer of 1975, there were only a handful of Asian public health inspectors working in British Columbia. The working environment in a big city was quite different from rural areas. Restaurant operators were always busy and rarely spent time talking leisurely, other than about the restaurant business. Whenever there is a contentious situation regarding the inspection, operators were quick to defend themselves and easily got upset. It may have been a way of bluffing during those days when operators were often saying (whether they mean it or not), "Don't talk to me. Talk to my lawyer." Operators had a faster pace and were not as willing to comply. This different attitude and circumstances took me a while to get used to. I had to change my approach and be very careful when I discussed problems with these operators. I had to make sure that I was correct in my decision and that my superior would support me. I didn't want to back-track my decision because my superior would not go along. I would lose my credibility, and even integrity.

Chapter 3

Consequences for saying 'NO' to the public

As a Public Health Inspector, we often have to say "no" to the public, and the response isn't always positive. The following are some anecdotes about how some operators have responded to an inspector's "no".

Being chased by a butcher holding a large knife during my practicum

At the beginning of the Public Health Program at B.C. Institute of Technology, I remember the Program Head Instructor told the class that a Public Health Inspector trainee was chased out by a butcher holding a knife during the beginning of the practicum. This incident really stayed in my mind during my entire career as a Public Health Inspector. I didn't want the same happen to me.

It is very easy for a new PHI practicum student to think, "I am the inspector" and automatically expect the public to respect and to comply with his or her demands. Something that I learned is that respect has to be earned. If your conduct and attitude are not respectful, you will not earn the public's trust and respect.

Being yelled at to get out during inspection

One of my colleagues was told to leave during his first inspection at a coffee and donut shop. Trying to prevent confrontation, this colleague did leave the premises. Because of such a negative initial reception and relationship, this inspector was never able to carry out his duties or even communicate properly with this operator. This inspector simply kept getting yelled at, time after time.

Whenever I have to deal with a new operator whose background I do not know much about, my first approach is to start at a much slower and mellower pace. This way, I am more likely to build up a better working relationship with the operator and will not get into confrontations right away. Of course, some operators will test or challenge you right at beginning.

Threat from a Barber

I had just started my new job on the North Shore and my first assignment was to inspect all the personal services in the area, such as hair salons, barbershops, and beauty parlours. The personal services were considered to be lowest in priority and therefore not inspected as frequently. It was the second week and about mid-morning when I walked into a barbershop in the West Vancouver Dundarave area. As I entered, I spotted the male operator, who was about 6'5" and ferocious looking. After I identified myself as a Public Health Inspector, I began to open the hair cutting station drawers to check if they were clean. Suddenly, I heard a very unfriendly voice with a threatening tone say, "I will throw you out the door if you touch the drawer one more time." At that time, I was more puzzled than afraid. I had to explain to the barber why I was opening the drawers, that it is part of my job. The barber may have tried to bluff this little young Chinese guy, but I was a stubborn Health Inspector. I toughed it up and managed to complete the inspection in the end.

Threat from a Butcher

After finishing my inspection of a medium-sized supermarket, I was leaving the back door trying to get to my car in the parking area. As I was exiting, I ran into a man coming out of a car lugging a pig carcass on his shoulder. He was walking toward the back door of the supermarket. I stopped him and asked what he was doing. He told me that he was going to drop off the carcass for 'meat-aging-process' in the walk-in-cooler of the supermarket. I noticed that there was no legend of approval stamp on the carcass and the man admitted that it was not approved by the meat inspector. I denied the man entry into the supermarket, stating that I would have to lay a charge against him if he did. The man was very upset and belligerent. He cursed and threatened to complain to the mayor. I told him to complain to the prime minister for all I cared. Eventually, the man left the supermarket and a warning was issued to the butcher of the supermarket regarding such illegal and unsafe practices.

Threat from a Restaurant Owner

One time at about eleven in the morning, I walked into a small restaurant and to do an inspection. The restaurant was very quiet with only a few customers drinking coffee. I was surprised and felt indignant because the operator impolitely asked me to come back to do the inspection another time without any valid reason. Of course, I did not back down, so I carried on. That operator followed me everywhere and cursed me with all kinds of obscenities. He finally called my Chief Public Health Inspector in the office. By this time, I had almost completed my inspection. My chief advised me by phone that it may be wise for me to leave the restaurant for my safety.

My inspection was done and I gave the inspection report to that angry operator and left the restaurant. I wasn't afraid while he was following me and cursing (maybe I didn't know what to be afraid of), because I was mandated to be there to do the inspection and was merely doing my job, performing my duty.

About two weeks later, I went back to the same restaurant for a re-inspection. I thought this operator would treat me with the same belligerent and un-co-operative attitude. To my surprise, he smiled and appeared to be receptive when I walked in. It was as if the previous animosity had not happened. During casual conversation at the end of my re-inspection, he told me that he was under a lot of pressure because of his financial situation. He was facing bankruptcy. That may be why he was so angry at the previous inspection.

Threat from a Delicatessen Operator

It was about ten in the morning and I had just walked into a small delicatessen, ready to do an inspection. The delicatessen was not busy, with only two or three customers having coffee. When I entered the kitchen, the male German operator told me right away in an unkind tone to come back another time. I asked why and no answer was given. Again, I felt that I was being challenged with no reason. I was slightly pushed by the operator, who tried to stop me doing the inspection. I was a little nervous, but felt that I had to do my job, so, I carried on and completed the inspection. It was probably not as thorough as I would like, but it was done to fulfill my duty.

I had to go back to the same delicatessen two or three weeks later. This time I expected the same rough reception, but amazingly this operator was much more co-operative. The previous yelling and pushing did not happen. At the end of the visit, the operator told me that the morning I inspected his shop earlier, I was the fourth government inspector that day. He had bad reports from the fire Inspector, plumbing inspector and building inspector. When I walked in, it was just too much for him to take and I was the unlucky inspector who came at the wrong time.

A Builder's lien on the Inspector's personal residence

In the early 1990s, a couple started a simple real estate transaction to purchase a piece of property on a popular small west coast island.

Then the nightmare began. This transaction later turned into a five-year Supreme Court case. This case involved the realtor, the real estate developer, the builder, the sewage disposal design engineer, the building inspector, and the public health inspector. The judgement found the health inspector involved had failed to carry out his duties in a proper manner and improperly permitted a health hazard in water and sewage disposal. I believe that a builder's lien was placed on this health inspector's personal residence later.

I learned from this incident that I needed to be even more careful to ensure diligence in my obligations when exercising my duty as a Public Health Inspector to prevent liability suits against me.

Tobacco Smoking Complaint

I had the bad habit of tobacco smoking during my school years at BCIT. I smoked during a pub night with some classmates after school and when attending parties. I continued the habit even when I was working in Redwater, Alberta, and believed that I was already addicted to nicotine, even though I was still a light smoker. I always craved the first puff in the morning and the rest was mainly a habit. I tried many times to quit, but temptations and easy access prevented me from kicking the addiction. I was fortunate to meet my wife and, with her support and encouragement, I succeeded in quitting.

Smoking complaints were common while I was an inspector, though today they are less of an issue because of public bans. I received an anonymous smoking complaint from a realty office near my office. The female complainant indicated that her manager smoked heavily inside his office. I know why she kept her complaint anonymous: obviously, she was afraid of her manager.

I went to the company, which was in a fairly small office. I identified myself and asked to see the manager. I was asked to wait, and after over twenty minutes, the manager with a stern face opened the door and showed me into his office. As soon as I walked in and sat down, I noticed a big glass ash tray filled with cigarette butts sitting on the desk. I could smell the smoke present in the office. After I sat down and introduced myself, I explained I was there to investigate the smoking complaint. It took me less than five minutes to explain to the manager that any indoor smoking was a violation with the City of North Vancouver Smoking By-law. To my surprise, right after my explanation, this manager stood up with an expressionless flat face and said, "Thank you". He opened the door and showed me out. It happened so quickly that I did not know what to say or how to react until I realized that I was outside and the door shut on me.

When I got back to my office and was trying to comprehend what happened, I wondered how I should follow up with this complaint. It took some effort to locate the regional office of this realty company, which was in the downtown Vancouver area. I talked to the regional manager by phone and informed him of this whole incident. I also followed up with a written letter to the regional manager and carbon copied it to the sub-office manager regarding the City of North Vancouver Smoking By-law, requesting remedy actions. To my surprise, after about a week, this sub-office manager called and was extremely apologetic to me regarding his improper behaviour during our meeting and promised that he would take action immediately to comply with the smoking by-law. I had no more smoking complaints from that realty office.

I know where you live and I am going to burn down your house

A female inspector colleague had some difficulties with a restaurant operator. After multiple inspections, a very negative relationship was formed between the inspector and the operator. One day, this operator told her with a threatening tone, "I know where you live and I am going to burn down your home." Scary, isn't it?

My personal belief is that while on the job, I need to be tactful, credible with integrity, sympathetic, reasonable, and also should not be easily bluffed by the operator. Of course, I am very thankful that not many serious incidents occurred during my career.

PETER K. P. LEE

Chapter 4

Funny Encounters

When I was training to be a Public Health Inspector at BCIT, there is only so much that can be covered during that time, and nothing in my training could prepare me for some of the following situations described next.

Shoe Odour Complaint

Odour complaints are often difficult to deal with. I remember one time, a young woman called to complain of an odour that was coming from her apartment. I was new on the job on the North Shore. With one other experienced PHI, I arrived at her apartment. As soon as we walked in, we noted there were many pairs of shoes on the floor at the entrance. We walked through her apartment and could not conclude where and what smell the young woman was complaining about. Eventually, I told her that we could not find the obvious source of the odour other than the leather smell from the shoes. I made that comment not to criticize her shoes, but simply to say they were the only odorous items that I could find during the inspection. Not surprisingly, the young woman was not content with our finding and I learned that she later complained to my Medical Health Officer about the comment. Maybe she felt that my comment suggested that she had stinky feet? The other inspector and I had to explain to our Medical Health Officer about the incident and no more action was needed.

We Don't Serve Silverfish Here

One time I received a complaint from a restaurant patron who spotted silverfish in a small French restaurant. This complainant had reported the sighting to a female restaurant staff member. The same complainant went back to the restaurant and was still seeing the silverfish. He was upset and believed that he was getting no response to his complaint, so he finally called my office. I investigated this matter and found that a new young female employee, who had just moved to the West Coast from Quebec, was working there as a waitress. During my investigation, I asked this waitress, "Do you have silverfish in the restaurant?" Her response was simply, "We do not serve silverfish here." This is a good example of miscommunication and misunderstanding. This young woman simply did not know what silverfish was and thought it was some kind of fish that she did not find or recognize on the restaurant's menu.

Silverfish is a common household insect, but is not considered to be a significant health concern. Silverfish are slender, wingless, scale-covered insects with a pair of long antennae and tail-like appendages at the end of the abdomen. They can grow to about half an inch long. This is a widespread pest that is commonly found in new apartments, dwellings, libraries, bakeries and other buildings, especially in warm and secluded places. They may be found on floors, walls, and in among papers, books, and clothing. It feeds on carbohydrates, starch, dextrin, and also substances containing protein, such as gum and glue.

Big People have Big Turds

A woman called my office regarding frequent blockages in her toilet and requested that I investigate. When I arrived at her apartment, I noted that she was a heavy set woman and at least six feet tall. Her husband was at least 6'5". The woman explained that they could find no obvious defect with the toilet, but it was frequently plugged. I noticed that it appeared to be fairly small. We carried on the investigation and conversation. Eventually, we concluded that the opening of the toilet was too small to handle the size of stools that she and her husband produced due to their body size. We concluded that "big people would naturally have big stools". After I left and was inside my car, I could not control myself any more. I laughed and laughed until tears ran down my face!

West Nile Virus and the Grave Digger:

In the early 2000s, the West Coast was monitoring the spreading of the West Nile Virus from the eastern provinces and the US. Each year the virus seemed to get closer and closer. In Ontario, it was causing quite a scare and there were fears of a larger outbreak. The virus' hosts are mainly the corvids, such as the ravens, crows, jays and magpies. As a monitoring program, from June to October, health authorities in the Metro Vancouver area picked up dead crows and ravens and sent them to the laboratory for testing.

It was Monday morning. Someone left a telephone message in my office requesting pickup of a dead crow from the caller's residence. When I arrived there, I found a huge, bushy yard and could not see anybody around. Eventually, after ringing and ringing the doorbell, I was prepared to leave. Just then, a middle-aged male opened the door. I started to ask the gentleman to see where the dead crow was so I could bring it back to the office for testing. With a stern face, he told me to follow him. When we arrived under a particular tree in the garden, he pointed down with his finger to a spot on the ground and told me that he buried the dead crows two days before. This gentleman handed me a shovel, which was leaning on the tree. He told me that I could dig out the dead crow myself. Of course, I did not dig it up because we would only pick up specimens that had been properly refrigerated in good condition. When I got back to my car, I didn't know if I should laugh or get angry with that whole incident. It seems I was promoted as a grave-digger.

A Pest Problem, Mr. Roach?

One time, I was attending a food exhibition in Vancouver Trade and Convention Centre and examined all the exhibiting booths. I stopped by a pest control company exhibit and spoke with the attendant regarding roach control. He gave me several informative handouts and introduced himself as Mr. Roach. I thought it was a gimmick that Mr. Roach worked in roach control, but I did not pay much attention. When I was finally ready to move on to another booth, he handed me his business card. I was so surprised that I did not know how to respond — his business card actually showed his last name as Roach. This was probably the only time that I came across someone with the right name for the right job. "Mr. Roach is here to eradicate the roaches!"

PETER K. P. LEE

Chapter 5

Interesting Assignments

There are times when the career is uneventful, but sometimes there are interesting assignments that come along to help me see my profession in a different light.

Being an Expert in Positive and Negative Situations

Several years after I worked on the North Shore (I forget the exact date), I was called into the Chief PHI's office and was given a special assignment. The Governor General of Canada was coming to the North Vancouver Burrard Drydock, a ship builder at the foot of Lonsdale, to launch a new ship.

The health services and inspection coverage normally would have been done by the Federal Health Protection Branch staff, but they were unavailable and turned it over to our office. When I walked in, I was thoroughly checked by the RCMP. I was the only food safety person in attendance.

The reception was put on by a reputable caterer in Vancouver and things went smoothly. That evening, I did not have a chance to see the event but stayed in the temporary kitchen in a back room of the Burrard Drydock, watching and checking the catering staff preparing and serving food. That evening, I really felt important, particularly when the catering staff asked for my advice on food preparation, and what to do and what not to do.

However, at another time, being an expert is not as pleasant as serving the Governor General of Canada. One day, the Medical Health Officer and the Chief PHI told me, with very short notice, to inspect and supervise a body exhumation in the District of North Vancouver Cemetery. The health regulation requires health approval with written permission by the Medical Health Officer and health official supervision for body exhumation. When I arrived at the cemetery, the funeral home limousine and staff were already on site, and the coffin was already dug up. I was to supervise the proper transfer of the coffin with the body into the limousine. It would then be shipped back to its final destination in Italy. My assignment was complete as soon as the limousine left the cemetery carrying the coffin. This was an unusual assignment and I had no forehand knowledge of what to do or what to look for. I was not given any instructions to supervise this exhumation and that's probably because no one would think that such a "Halloween assignment" would be part of a PHI's job description to begin with.

What to Expect at a Nudist Swimming Pool

I was called into the chief's office and given an assignment to check out a nudist club on Mountain Highway in the District of North Vancouver. This private nudist club was founded in late 1930s. Apparently, there was a swimming pool in this colony that our office was not aware of and was never inspected. In fact, this colony was not known at all until that time, though I believe it is still in operation at the time of this writing. I called the president of the nudist club and a date was set for a meeting and inspection. I remember it was early summer, perhaps early June, and the weather was fairly warm. I really did not know what to look for or what I would find when I got there. I drove as far as the road could take me and after about half an hour of hiking into the bush, I finally reached the camp. Before I headed out for the inspection, the other inspectors in the office joked that I would see a lot of naked beautiful women. To my surprise when I arrived at the club, I met the two gentlemen, the club president and caretaker, fully clothed with no naked women around. I was also surprised to see that the so-called swimming pool was simply a big hole on the ground with no filtration, circulation, or chlorination system. In the end, I had to hike back to my car with a not-so-desirable report for the chief because they need to be in compliance with the swimming pool regulations. As far as I know, there was no other follow up. Anti-climactic, isn't it?

Destruction of contaminated liquor:

One time we had a very heavy rainfall on the North Shore that created a lot of flooding for many businesses, including a government liquor store in West Vancouver. The Health Department and the store management decided to pull $50,000 worth of liquor off the shelves due to potential flood water contamination through the bottle caps. It was to be disposed of in the North Vancouver landfill at the end of Premier Street.

I arrived at the landfill at the arranged time and saw cases and cases of Johnny Walker, whisky, rum, brandy, and others piled into one area. At the end, a bulldozer with huge steel wheels operated by the landfill staff was running over the cases of liquor until all the bottled liquors were crushed and destroyed. I could smell the aroma of the different types of liquor in the air. I was never a drinker and maybe I was picked because the chief knew that I would be able to complete this task neutrally. Maybe an appreciator of liquor would find this assignment a tragic waste!

Anthrax Incidents: Then and Now

1975. It was my first year working on the North Shore. The Chief PHI advised me to respond to a call that some camel yarn was contaminated with anthrax in a yarn store on Lower Lonsdale. At that time, I did not really know what Anthrax was, other than it is classified as a communicable disease. I and one other inspector went to the yarn shop to investigate the yarn, which was imported from either India or Nepal. In the end, the Chief PHI asked us to seize the contaminated yarn, so I put it in the trunk of my car without any proper containers or packaging.

We handled it by simply covering our hands inside common brown paper bags. When we got back to the office, the Chief PHI decided to put all the contaminated yarn into the ordinary 70 litre galvanized garbage cans (there was enough for two or three cans). After all the commotion settled down, we realized the potential danger that I and the other inspector were exposed to. The Chief PHI gave me a can of Lysol as a disinfectant to spray the trunk of my car. To do the job properly and safely, we should have had special clothing and gloves and even a respirator, and it should not have been collected unprotected into my car. The other health inspector and I wound have easily contracted anthrax, which is a deadly communicable disease. A special HazMat unit with Darth Vader-style suits and masks would have been appropriate, but they did not exist in those days. The Chief PHI was interviewed by the local newspaper in the next few days, and a picture of him in his office with the garbage cans full of yarn was in the paper. I believe that this yarn was sent to the laboratory and tested negative for anthrax.

This next story happened at least thirty years after the previous anthrax Incident involving the contaminated yarn.

I was always reluctant to act for the boss in their absence because I felt I was black-listed and would not have a chance for any upward promotion, no matter how much extra effort I put in. I would receive a few dollars more in pay for acting for the boss, but I would also expose myself to much more responsibility and demands. It was simply not worth it for me.

This time I was pressured into acting for the boss as Acting Chief PHI for three days. On the last day of it at about 3 pm, the Medical Health Officer (MHO) walked into my office and informed me that a mysterious white powder was left in the North Vancouver Police Station. He requested that I respond right away.

In the 2000s, the bio-terrorism threat in the United States and Canada was very prevalent. Government agencies in the U.S. and Canada treated bio-terrorism threats very seriously. An extensive response protocol and guidelines involving many governmental agencies was put in place. I was aware of bio-terrorism, but not fully aware of the policy and guidelines in detail because I was just acting for the chief for a few days. I asked the MHO for advice on how I should tackle this assignment in the next fifteen minutes. The MHO left my office, but returned in a few minutes to drop off the "Bio-Terrorism Response Guidelines" folder on my desk. He asked me to review it and deal with the white powder threat. This unfamiliar, big, thick guideline book, with at least thirty pages, was supposed to give me the knowledge to resolve this assignment within the next thirty minutes.

Thank God that with some logical and critical thinking, I was able to resolve this threat amicably with the police and fire chief. I just used common sense to deal with this matter. We all agreed that this incident did not qualify as a 'credible threat'. However, this powder was eventually collected by a special police squad unit and shipped to a testing laboratory in Winnipeg, Manitoba. I was not aware of the lab result and I assumed it likely tested negative for anthrax.

In both situations dealing with anthrax, simplified and clearer guidelines for the investigation protocol would be more helpful for the inspectors.

Feces Counting Officer

PHIs are known to collect and pick up stool samples for lab testing frequently especially after suspect food poisoning or communicable disease incidents. In our office, PHIs are often jokingly called Feces Collecting Officers.

I have done many different tasks in this career, but never thought that I would get a new job title as a Dog Feces Counting Officer. The Chief asked me to go into his office for a new assignment. Due to the many public complaints received by the city hall regarding dog feces accumulation problems in the dog walking trail in the West Vancouver 'Ambleside-Sea-Wall' area beside the CN Rail (Canadian National Rail) rail-track, my assignment was to walk through the sea-wall area to observe and to determine how bad the dog dropping situation is. In the end, in order for me to fulfill this assignment, I took a note pad in my hand and started walking and counting dog droppings on the dog walking trail beside the railway track. I walked for about 2 or 3 kilometres and counted about 400 droppings on the dog walking trail. That night when I was resting at home in my bed, my mind was vividly filled with the image of dog droppings of different size, colour, and shape!

Making Medical History in Canada...With More Droppings

In early January, 1987, I received a communicable disease report from the provincial laboratory indicating that a child tested positive for Salmonella falkensee. The enteric bacteriology laboratories serotyped a Salmonella falkensee, a variety new to British Columbia. This identification was confirmed by the National Enteric Reference Centre at the Laboratory Centre for Disease Control in Ottawa, which also identified it as a new serotype in Canada.

During the follow-up investigation, I found that this child's mother was a veterinary assistant and his father was a longshoreman. There was no history of recent foreign travel or immigration, nor exotic pets.

On February 24, 1987, the child's father called me back and advised that he remembered finding at work an iguana the previous December, which had accidently been brought aboard a ship from South America. He rescued the iguana and brought it home as a pet for a couple of days. The iguana was later given to friends, but was then returned to the initial family. As this iguana was the only unusual finding in the family history, it was determined worthwhile to investigate its fecal droppings for this rare salmonella serotype. On February 27, 1987, Salmonella falkensee was subsequently isolated and identified by the enteric lab, two months after the initial isolation from the child. This slate-coloured iguana with a spiny tail, Ctenosaura hemilopha, eventually found a home in the Vancouver Aquarium.

This investigation reviewed the first diarrheal illness caused by Salmonella falkensee in Canada. This strain was also isolated from a South American iguana (Ctenosaura hemilpha), which had briefly been a pet at the family home. To the best of my knowledge at the time of the investigation, this was the first reported case of salmonella transmission from an iguana to a person in Canada.

PETER K. P. LEE

Lions Gate Bridge and vehicle traffic pollution

A governmental low rental and senior housing project is located very close to the Lions Gate Bridge. One particular senior woman was complaining about all kinds of problems and was becoming a pain in the neck.

One day, she called again regarding black dust outside. She said she could not open her window and was having a hard time breathing. I arrived at her unit and found no obvious environmental concerns. While talking to her, she concluded that the Lions Gate Bridge and the vehicle traffic was the culprit. The noise and dust bothered her so much that she practically demanded I remove and relocate the Lions Gate Bridge. I got a picture in my mind of the headlines that would cause in the newspaper.

At the end of the investigation, I explained to the woman that there really was not much I could do with this complaint. I suggested she contact the Department of Transport, which has jurisdiction over the Lions Gate Bridge. I guess they couldn't do much for her because the Lions Gate Bridge is still here.

"Green Washing"?

Would you like your white clothing, linens, and bathroom surfaced dyed green free of charge?

From the 1970s to the early 90s on the North shore, residents often complained about a white laundry coming out greenish. There were also complaints about green stains on bathtubs. This kind of complaint mainly came from new residents who just moved to the North Shore.

Our water supply was mainly coming from the local rivers such as Seymour River, Capilano River, and Lynn Creek. Because of the organic materials from the river and reservoir, our water supply is naturally acidic. The PH of the water coming out of the tap will read about 6.8, which is on the acidic side.

The green was caused by a chemical reaction between our acidic water and the copper water pipes. This chemical reaction could change white fabrics to a greenish color during laundering and caused a greenish stain on porcelain bathroom fixtures. The stain problem is particularly severe if the porcelain fixtures had a leaky tap.

Experimenting with one complainant regarding the greenish color of the laundry, we found certain brands of detergents to be more problematic. Many local residents were aware of the acidic nature of the water supply and did not complain. It was recommended to residents to run the tap water until it is cold first thing in the morning, and to avoid drinking the water because the chemical reaction could cause lead and copper to leach into the water around the soldered joints in the copper pipes.

Now the buffering process of the GVRD or Metro Vancouver should improve the situation with the green stains because this water treatment process brings up the PH level of the water, making it less acidic.

Public Health Inspector, Animal Control Officer also?

It is hard to believe that a public health inspector could also be an animal control officer. Because of the potential for rabies, health inspectors are involved when a dog bite incident occurs. Rabies is under the BC Communicable Disease Control jurisdiction. Often the dog bite victim will report the incident to the police or by-law officer, and then the Health Department is eventually contacted.

Whenever a dog bite report is received, a health inspector is to confirm whether the victim's skin is broken, which is a potential mode of transmission of rabies. The health inspector will issue a letter requesting the dog involved to be confined within the dog owner's property for ten days. Both the health inspector and the by-law officer will check on the confinement compliance.

This kind of incident often drags the inspector into a rough and contentious situation between the victim and the dog owner. Often the victim would call for putting the dog to sleep. I have seen a few dog bite incidents in which young children got hurt quite badly. For example, if a dog bite results in 20-30 stitches in the hospital, I can appreciate why the parent of the victim would be very upset and demand immediate action of putting the dog to sleep.

Public Health Inspector: *bill collector also?*

Prior to 2008, many health permit fees and pool permit fees were outstanding and operators were simply not paying them. There was no recourse from the health authority. Hundreds of thousands of dollars in outstanding permit fees simply waived every year.

This was changed in 2008. From 2008 to 2011, my last years of working prior to my retirement, all health inspectors became permit fee collectors. Health inspectors were to call the operators directly by phone or in person requesting the outstanding permit fees to be paid.

Health inspectors were to advise operators of an additional administration permit fee and eventually enforce closure if it was not paid. Most of my colleagues and I were not comfortable with this additional role as a tax collector. We felt this was not in our job description as public health inspectors, but we did it anyway to the best of our ability, without damaging the positive relationships we had with operators.

I remember returning to the office at the end of the day with cheques and a fair sum of cash, including coinage. I felt like I was back to the old days when the transit bus driver was strapped with a metal coinage belt on the waist to collect fares from passengers. Because of this consistent fee collection practice, the outstanding permit fees were drastically reduced. The operators finally got the message that permit fees must be paid on time prior to the expiry date at the end of March each year. This new assignment did create some displeasure and uncomfortable relationships between us, health inspectors, and the restaurant operators.

Public Health Inspector to clean up the bus-stop cigarette butts?

One time the chief public health inspector and the senior public health inspector were summoned urgently by the mayor, asking them to come to his office right away. The rest of the health inspectors in our office speculated on what would call for such a short notice meeting.

Later, when the chief and the senior PHI returned, they both expressed disbelief for the purpose of the meeting. Apparently, it had to do with the cigarette butts in the bus stops near by the municipal hall.

The mayor was not pleased with all these cigarette butts in the bus stop areas and wanted them removed. We couldn't believe that the mayor would request the chief and senior public health inspectors to deal with this. So, now our job description should include cleaning cigarette butts with brooms and wheelbarrows at bus stops? The reasonable solution was to call the municipal public works department instead because there are staff members there who would be upset if we took away their jobs!

Soft Ice Cream and Beaches

What do soft ice cream and beaches have in common? Maybe people would automatically think of lazy summer days, eating ice cream and enjoying the beach. Most people wouldn't think that these were once the monitoring duties of a Public Health Inspector.

It was a routine task to collect soft ice cream samples in the summer during the two years I worked in Redwater, Alberta. Regular sampling of soft ice cream was carried out at least once a month. The samples were then sent to the provincial laboratory in Edmonton for routine testing of total coliform, fecal coliform, and standard plate count. If the lab results were not satisfactory, a health inspector would issue a closure order for the soft ice cream machine. A resampling procedure would be carried out after the machine was thoroughly cleansed and disinfected. If the lab result was satisfactory, then the soft ice cream machine would be put back in operation.

It was pleasant to carry out this sampling task by going in and out of the walk-in-cooler, which is cool compared to the hot outside weather in the prairie summer. Collecting the soft-ice-cream mix with a glass suction jet-tube was sticky and messy. When using this jet-tube, one end had to be dipped inside a plastic package of liquid soft ice cream mix, then a glass tube wrapped in a rubber sieve was broken by hand to provide enough suction to collect the ice cream mix into a sampling glass tube. When I came back to work on the North Shore, this soft ice cream sampling was still carried on a little longer, but was eventually discontinued due to budget concerns.

PETER K. P. LEE

When I started working on the North Shore, it was an enjoyable task to collect beach water samples during the summer months in Panorama Park, Myrtle Park, and Ambleside Park. I remember that I had to put on knee-high rubber boots and wade out to the beach up to about a foot of water. I used a wooden rod, which has a metal clamp at the end to hold a water sampling glass bottle during the collection of the beach water.

This wooden rod is an ordinary homemade wooden stick about five feet long and is nothing high tech. I believe that this particular wooden stick was made by a former chief public health inspector. Every time I did beach sampling, swimmers and sun-bathers would watch me with a peculiar look on their faces, wondering what on Earth was I doing. The beach water samples were then sent to the provincial laboratory for routine testing for total coliform and fecal coliform. If the lab result was not satisfactory, the health department issued a closure order for the beach, which would be placarded with a health warning. Resampling would take place and the beach would remain closed until a satisfactory result is obtained.

Depending on the source of the coliform and the ocean current, the closure may remain for a long time. I remember the unpleasant reception from the life-guards and the public when I had to put a closure sign on the beach. People called the health department and complained about the beach being closed, even when the water looked clean. This beach sampling program was eventually discontinued by the health department, but carried on by the Greater Vancouver Regional District (GVRD), which was later renamed Metro Vancouver.

The last Squatter House on the Maplewood Mud Flats, District of North Vancouver?

In the 1970s, a large number of hippies took up residence in the illegal old and dilapidated housing in the Dollarton Highway area, referred to as the Maplewood Mud Flats. Eventually, the District of North Vancouver Council ordered all residents to vacate the area. The buildings were set ablaze by the fire department.

One time in 1979, I was accompanying the chief PHI to visit an illegal squatted house located close to the old Crab Shack on Dollarton Highway in North Vancouver. When we arrived, we found a shanty shack hidden behind the thick bush. This shack was built just on top of McCartney Creek, which is a small creek running out to the open beach. This shack had no sewage or water services and was put together with pieces of old recycled lumber. It was a house for one very old man in at least his late 80s. Inside this shack, you could see and hear creek water running below through small gaps of the wooden floor.

This old man had been living there alone for many years and at the time of our visit, he appeared healthy. At the end, the chief and I saw what we needed to see and left. This house should have been demolished the same way as the others, but because of his old age, he was left alone. Everyone hoped that this old man would die of old age, then the old shack could be demolished. I believe my boss would have discussed the findings of this visit with the local government, but I did not know what decision was made or what went on.

A few years after, I was driving by this old shanty shack and found it was gone. I didn't know what had happened to the old man, but I was sure that everyone was glad this illegal squatter shack was finally gone for good. This location is now part of the Maplewood Bird Sanctuary and the original Crab Shack was demolished and relocated twice at the time of this writing.

If Your Child Gets a Sunburn, Do You Ban the Sun?

There are some parents who, in an attempt to help their child feel better after falling down, would blame the ground for making the child fall down. The following are incidents that demonstrate this kind of thinking.

An irate father called and complained that his young daughter's body had broken out into many bad rashes after swimming in a municipal swimming pool in North Vancouver. He was initially not aware of his daughter's extreme sensitivity to chlorine, but it was later confirmed by a family doctor. Of course, this father was very angry because of this incident and, unfortunately, I happened to answer the telephone. I got

PETER K. P. LEE

an earful, being accused of not taking steps to protect the public. At the end of the telephone conversation, he demanded that I close the swimming pool and order the pool manager to stop using chlorine to disinfect the water. Chlorine, because of its effectiveness, has always been recommended by the Health Department for disinfecting swimming pool water. This father never accepted or even considered that it was his daughter's unusually extreme sensitivity to the chlorine that caused these bad rashes. Our task is to protect the general public health, but not individual health. Perhaps the best solution for this complaint would be to make sure his daughter does not swim in any chlorinated pools in the future.

In another situation, a man called my office and complained that his electric stovetop was too hot to touch and considered this dangerous for his young children at home. This caller believed that the stovetop should be cold and not hot.

I believe some newer electric stoves with no exposed coil on top are cool to touch outside the cooking area. This caller had the older design that is hot to touch on the top surface, especially after the grill is turned on for a length of time. I wonder when people like this will realize that salt is salty, sugar is sweet, and a stove is naturally hot. This caller forgot that it should be his responsibility to teach his children that a stove is hot and should not be touched to avoid burns.

Chapter 6

Foodborne Illness

Food poisoning!

The public often expects the public health inspector to be able to tell them instantly if questionable food is safe or not, like a dip stick test on a car. Unfortunately, we do not have a magic wand to determine if the food is good or bad. It is a complex and time-consuming procedure that normally takes at least three or four days in the laboratory. The laboratory will look for common foodborne illness organisms such as Salmonella, Staphylococcus, Campylobacter, Yersinia, and fecal bacteria such as Escherchia coli and the heterotrophic plate count.

To confirm a food poisoning incident, the following samples are needed: (1) leftover suspect food items ideally right from the complainant's dinner plate, (2) a stool sample or a vomitus sample from the complainant and (3) same suspect food from the restaurant. All these samples are submitted to the laboratory for testing and if the results are positive and matched with the same organism, then we have a positive confirmation. Without the confirmation, the incident would normally be classified as suspect foodborne illness.

Sometimes a complainant would claim a doctor told them that they had food poisoning without any laboratory specimen testing. When the complainant called, they had already determined in their mind that food poisoning was the case because their doctor said so. This often created a lot of confusion for the complainant, making the investigation very difficult and even creating unnecessary conflicts with the public health inspector.

Raw Food and food poisoning?

Through curiosity and adventurousness, people often want to try unfamiliar or ethnic foods. They often assume that all food for sale in the market is edible raw or cooked, and pay no attention to the instructions prior to eating. Consumers need to pay attention to the nature and characteristics of unfamiliar foods prior to sampling. Raw or undercooked foods such as raw oyster, eggs cooked sunny side up and sashimi will definitely pose a higher health risk as a source of foodborne illness. It is a general rule of thumb that the "rarer the food, the higher the health risk." My professional opinion is to have no sympathy for anyone who gets sick after eating raw or undercooked food because it was their choice.

Too Much of a Good Thing

I had a luxury seafood buffet floating boat restaurant in my area. During the 1980s, the cost of a seafood buffet there would be about $28 per person. It included cold and hot dishes with over forty different types of seafood to choose from, including raw oysters, octopus, lobsters and king-crabs. I remember receiving foodborne illness complaints from the customers of this seafood boat fairly frequently, around once every few months. I must say that the sanitation of this restaurant was always well-kept with no obvious health problems. Looking back now, I wonder how many of those suspected foodborne illness complaints were not really food poisoning but simply eating too much protein-rich seafood in a short time.

I believe that because the cost of the meal was so high, when customers see so many different types of seafood in front of them, they want to sample everything. Seafood is very rich in protein and when customers overload on it, they would get stomach cramps, diarrhea, and even vomiting. Most people want to eat their money's worth. Of course, some of these food poisoning complaints may also come from a seafood allergy.

A recent study by the Food Allergy and Anaphylaxis Network (FAAN) that surveyed more than 15,000 people showed over 3.5% of people are now believed to be affected by one or more food allergies. Finfish and shellfish allergies are fairly common. This famous seafood buffet boat was eventually closed down due to problems in renewing the lease.

Some people get "too much of a good thing" confused with "food borne illness."

Cassava (*tuberous root*)

One time a woman called regarding a burning sensation on her tongue and throat after eating raw cassava root. Cassava is a tuberous root of a plant and is very popular in specialty cuisine in some restaurants. Cassava is meant to be eaten after proper cooking and is very soft in texture and delicious. Sometimes, Cassava is simply eaten after boiling.

This woman purchased the cassava for the first time and ate it raw, treating it as a salad. Cassava contains natural cyanide and will cause side effects if consumed raw. This woman just wanted to try out something new and did not pay attention to the cooking instructions before eating. For safety and to avoid unexpected results, consumers should always read the cooking instructions before trying out a new and unfamiliar food.

Chapter 7

Chinese-Style Barbecued Meat Products
(roasted pig, Chinese style BBQ pork, chicken and duck,)

Starting in the mid-1970s, it was headline news of the back and forth between the Vancouver Health Department and the Vancouver Chinese-Style Barbecue Meat Merchants Association regarding the display temperature of these products in the Vancouver Chinatown area. The Vancouver Health Department required all cooked BBQ meat products to be displayed at a minimum of sixty degrees Celsius at all times. The meat merchants insisted that this temperature would dry the meat products and eventually they would become like wood chips, thereby destroying the intended taste and quality. They insisted that this two thousand-year-old practice was safe. At about the same time, Toronto was also dealing with this issue.

In September 1977, a grandfather purchased a Chinese-style BBQ meat product still warm at 11 AM, then went on a long bus trip. He arrived in Kingston, Ontario, at 5 PM. It is obvious that the ignorance of the consumer about keeping the meat at Danger Zone Temperatures for six hours after purchase created a health problem. Consuming food that have been in such conditions means that you would be consuming the great number of pathogens that would have multiplied during this time, resulting in food borne illness symptoms such as fever, chills, nausea, headaches, vomiting, stomach cramps, and diarrhea.

In 2001, the Hong Kong Food and Environmental Hygiene Department conducted a survey on Chinese-style BBQ and roasted meat products and found only one out of 406 roasted pig samples contained unsatisfactory levels of salmonella spp. Only two samples showed unsatisfactory E. coli levels due to unsatisfactory hygiene, improper handling, and sub-optimal storage conditions.

In Toronto in 2002, thirty-seven roasted pig samples were collected from thirty-five premises and analysed over eighteen days. All samples had acceptable counts for coliform, Bacillus cereus, E. coli, and Clostridium perfringens. No samples showed Salmonella and Campylobacter. This confirmed that thoroughly processed roasted pig is generally free of foodborne illness pathogens for the first five hours after roasting and therefore safe to consume, even when on display at ambient temperatures.

From mid-1970s, the Provincial Health Department and the Federal Health Protection Branch were dragged into this matter as well. Some prominent provincial and federal politicians were showing support for the Chinese BBQ meat merchants. One prominent Lower Mainland food microbiologist reviewed the Chinese-style barbequing method and believed the meat products were safe, and supported the Chinese BBQ Meat Merchants Association.

Discussions, negotiations, and health closure order threats went on and on between the Vancouver Health Department and the Chinese BBQ Meat Merchants Association. They came up with some improvements, such as enclosed display cases, heat lamps, and improved sanitary practices for the staff to prevent cross contamination.

Being a Chinese Canadian myself, I too enjoy eating these delicious products, especially the roasted pig's crispy and crunchy skin, wonderful aroma, and taste. I am aware that the turnover rate of the products is very fast. If not, they would be self-limiting in quality and no one would buy them. BBQ meat products are often replenished every couple of hours. The BBQ chef has to control the quantity of the product to ensure the freshness.

During some special Chinese festivities, these BBQ meat products are often sold out and customers line up sometimes thirty feet out the door. If these meat products are required to be displayed at a minimum of sixty degrees at all times, it would make them unpalatable and no one would buy them. I personally believe the Chinese BBQ products displayed at

PETER K. P. LEE

an ambient temperature for five or six hours are microbiologically safe. I believe that hygiene, such as good hand washing techniques, proper sanitary handling, and equipment sanitizing to prevent post-processing contamination are very important as well. Of course, the public needs to know that Chinese BBQ meat products or any ready-to-eat perishable foods need to be consumed as soon as possible.

Several months before my retirement, the Vancouver Coastal Health started a meat-sampling program for these products. Due to my retirement, I do not know if the result of that sampling program was positive or negative. One thing for sure is that I am very glad that even though I was working as a public health inspector, I was not working in the City of Vancouver with all these contentious issues. I was not directly dragged into this uneasy and difficult battle. At the same time, these Chinese BBQ meat products were not in demand on the North Shore and therefore did not present a problem to me.

Chapter 8

Food Odour Complaints

Coffee Bean Roasting

A popular coffee shop roasted its own bean several times a week inside the cafe. It was located in a commercial area with several condos in the back lane. Every time they did some roasting, the residents in the condos complained about the strong smell.

Normally, coffee drinkers would have loved the strong coffee aroma. The complaints carried on for a long period and several solutions were tried, but did not satisfy the residents. The Greater Vancouver Regional District (GVRD) air pollution control was involved and indicated some fumes involved were known to be toxic. Eventually, an expensive $15,000, after-burner vent was installed on the roof, which was supposed to reduce the level of the toxic fumes to a safe limit. The residents kept on complaining. The coffee shop finally opened up a new roasting facility in an industrial area that was non-residential. The odour complaints finally stopped.

Pizza smell in the public library

The librarian of the public library called complaining of pizza smells coming into the building. It was obvious when I arrived at the library to investigate. At that time, I personally found the pizza smell very appetizing and pleasant. A pizza operation was in the back lane across from the library. The air-intake of the library happened to be in the path of the exhaust air duct of the pizza place. Under certain weather and wind conditions, it was possible that the pizza smell could enter directly into the library air-intake. To solve this complaint, a solution was suggested to the library to relocate the air-intake to be far away from the exhaust duct of the restaurant. I believe the library did modify its air-intake system and I did not hear any more complaints.

Iranian Food Odour

An Iranian restaurant was located in the downtown commercial zone. Some self-owned condo apartment units were in the back lane behind it. Initially, the residents complained about the excessive noise coming from the motor of the ventilation system on the roof.

The district inspector spent several nights testing the noise levels with a noise meter. The noise by-law indicates that noise has to be within a certain level, but this was found to be within the acceptable limit. When the residents realized the noise wasn't illegal, they changed the direction and pursued a complaint against the odour of the Iranian food. This complaint went to the city council and some councillors wanted to have an odour by-law to deal with the odour problem in the municipality. The proposed by-law created some interest from the city council of the eastern provinces as well.

I am glad this did not materialize. If it was passed, I believe that a health inspector would have difficulty coming up with an instrument or meter that would be able to measure the objectionable odours. My opinion is that smell is so subjective. What is considered an offensive odour to someone can be very nice and pleasant to another. Foods such as cheese, yogurt, durian fruit and "stinky-tofu" often have strong and objectionable odours, but if you like them, then they would be considered a delicacy.

Chapter 9

Assignments involving people with mental illness

A middle-aged woman was noted by her neighbours for never taking her garbage out. The neighbors decided to call my office to express their concerns of garbage accumulating in this woman's home.

I investigated the complaint and, according to the neighbors, the woman lived alone, had a fairly decent and clean appearance, and did grocery shopping frequently. The neighbours indicated that they had not seen garbage taken out from her home for disposal for the last several months. They were concerned about the sanitary conditions inside the house and the woman's mental state. During my inspection, the woman was not home. I peeked through an open window in the basement and I saw piles of plastic grocery shopping bags on the table and on the floor. The neighbors also advised me that this woman in the past had shown indications of phobia to Asians. I was glad to learn about this woman's phobia.

To avoid unnecessary conflict, this complaint was handled by a colleague who is not Asian. The conclusion of this event was that this woman had some mental illness involving grocery shopping habits. She was shopping four or five times a day and would simply leave the groceries in the house upstairs and downstairs without even opening them. Some of the perishable foods were rotted beyond recognition. Fortunately, most were wrapped in plastic bags, so the smell was somewhat reduced. Eventually, this woman had to seek psychiatric help through the referral of the public health nurse. All the accumulated mountains of groceries were cleaned out by a municipal work crew. Of course, the cost for removing the accumulated groceries would be added to her property tax the following year.

A mental case involving Bed Bugs

I received a phone call from an apartment manager in West Vancouver indicating a female tenant had complained several times about a bed bug problem in her apartment. The manager requested many times with advance notice to check the bed bug situation, but was always refused entry by the tenant. The manager called me, hoping that I would be able to gain entry.

A meeting to inspect the unit was arranged. An appointment was made by the manager and the female tenant agreed. When the manager, his wife, and I arrived at the door, the female tenant only consented to allow me in, but not the manager and his wife. I went in alone. Inside, her apartment was fairly disorganized but clean. A stack of books was piled on the dining table in the kitchen. Simple bedding with linen was laid on the living room carpet floor. This tenant was so afraid of the bed bugs that she was sleeping on her living room floor instead of her bed. She showed me two spots on her hand and kept saying that she felt the bites from the bugs. I checked her bed and the sheet on it and found no signs of the bed bugs or any blood stains. I asked to turn up the bed so I could examine the mattress and the bed frame, but was refused by the tenant. I came out of the apartment and advised the manager that there were no obvious signs of bed bugs. I did indicate that the tenant would not allow me to check the mattress and the bed frame.

After I got back to my office, I reflected that this tenant behaved irrationally and may be considered mentally ill. I decided to call a mental health nurse and a social worker to see if they were aware of this person. The mental health nurse did not find any file record, but did believe this female tenant may have some mental problems. The nurse did try to meet with this tenant, but was also refused entry.

In the meantime, the apartment manager filed an eviction application and a notice was issued. Another three weeks went by and I received a call from the sheriff's office indicating that he was to exercise his duty to evict this female tenant. I pictured this woman sitting on the street with all her belongings scattered outside her apartment. It was not a pleasant thought and I was glad that I did not have to do the eviction. Another week passed and I was in the same apartment area so I stopped and talked to the manager, who advised me that the tenant's twin sister was finally reached and was able to move her and her belongings to another place. I was glad that the ugly eviction scene did not happen.

Suicidal Telephone Call

An elderly woman was physically healthy and lived alone in a government-subsidized senior's complex. Another health inspector and I had a history of dealing with her. She always complained of bugs such as silverfish and flying insects, and weird noises in her apartment. Every time we visited the unit, we found it to be very clean. We did find two or three dead insects in her bedding. She always wanted us to check the foundation of her bed and the chesterfield's upholstery. She always closed the windows even though they all had good screens. She even went as far as putting towels and linens under the door, thinking that would stop the bugs from entering her apartment.

One day, this woman called and left a message on my voicemail. She was again complaining of bugs in her unit and she was very frustrated and afraid. She said she didn't know what to do anymore and perhaps, she said, "I should kill myself." Those words really scared me. I had worked as a health inspector for about thirty-three years at this time, but I was never involved in a situation with somebody who wanted to commit suicide. I called back within an hour and had a long talk with her, mainly listening to her problem over and over again. At the end of that conversation, I told the woman not to give up hope and that I would get back to her with more help shortly.

I knew I had to take some appropriate action to deal with this woman.

Immediately after hanging up the phone, I contacted the senior home administrator of the housing complex and requested she check out the matter and also to check on the safety of the woman. I also contacted the public health nursing manager and then the mental health nurse. The mental health nurse checked her file and found this woman's mental illness records right away. According to her, this woman had threatened suicide in the past, and said she would deal with it. Anyway, I was somewhat at ease because this incident was referred to the proper channel and the woman was taken care of.

PETER K. P. LEE

Chapter 10

Noise and Garbage Complaints

Loud music from a local night club

There was a nightclub in West Vancouver right on Marine Drive with apartment residences across the back lane. Noise complaints were received during the summer nights while residents slept with the windows opened. The nightclub normally operated until 2 AM nightly. The parking lot was in the back lane area and every time a club-goer left through the back entrance, loud music escaped. I remember taking noise level readings in the back lane until two or three o'clock in the morning. It sure was a tiring and sleepy task. Eventually, the city council was involved and restricted the business hours. That nightclub went out of business in the end and noise problems were again resolved.

Train Noise

Two railroad companies operated right through the North Shore, District of North Vancouver, City of North Vancouver, and West Vancouver. Wherever the railway tracks were near a residential area, we would receive noise complaints the loud whistles, sharp wheel squealing, and heavy shunting noises. The City of North Vancouver was particularly bad because the grain elevator was so close to one section of residences near Low Level Road. City councillors, noise control officers from the health department, department of transport officials, and local representatives formed a committee to deal with this rail noise. These issues involved several governmental jurisdictions, including municipal, provincial, and federal transport departments.

Personally, I was not sympathetic with the complainants. The railway tracks were there long before residents were determined to live near that area, so people should have been aware of the noise emanating from the rail operation prior to moving there. Other than some enhanced maneuvering and handling of the rail operation, the noise level can only be reduced a little, and the problem would not disappear. The complainant would not accept that the trains are required by regulation to blow the whistle when approaching the crossing. I remember that to show the nearby complaining residents that the health department was dealing with the noise complaint, I spent many nights in the rain and cold, standing outside on the roadside and in back lanes taking noise level measurements.

Again, the permanent solution to resolve this noise issue, which will never happen, was either for the complainants to move out or to remove the railway tracks and stop the whole operation.

HVAC noise from the Recreation Centre

Imagine you're a police officer doing your rounds in the middle of the night and you spot a person holding a gun-like object in his hand walking around. What would you think he is doing?

A high-rise apartment resident in West Vancouver was complaining the HVAC noise was bothering him at night. This complainant believed that the HVAC noise was emanating from the West Vancouver Recreation Centre mainly at about mid-night. I remember the recreation maintenance superintendent and I were taking noise levels in the surrounding area from midnight to one in the morning. A policeman was cruising in his car and spotted me walking and pointing with the hand-held noise meter. The police stopped to see what I was doing. After my boring explanation he drove off. Obviously he had better things to do. That night, by the time I got home, it was about three in the morning and I was very tired. I slept as soon as I got to the bed.

PETER K. P. LEE

Another time, I was investigating a noise and dust complaint from a construction site. After I arrived there, I eventually met and talked with the site superintendent. I explained the nature of the complaint and the role of the city noise by-law. He was obviously irritated and unhappy to hear all the accusations. He was trying to deny and dispute everything that I said. Well, I did the preliminary investigation and had no choice but to leave. When I got back to my office, the first thing I did was to call the city hall engineering department regarding this complaint. I was trying to get the city engineer or building inspector involved because the city issued the building permit to this project. The next day, I had a phone message indicating the land developer of this job site called and wanted to apologize for the problems caused by this construction site. Apparently, the city engineering department got in touch with the land developer regarding the complaint and demanded remedy actions. I guess that in situations like this, the land developer wanted to be in good terms with the city hall and will pay more attention rather than dealing with a public health inspector. In the same afternoon, the superintendent left a message apologizing for the improper actions of the workmen and said he would take immediate actions to correct the noise and dust problem.

The above incidents indicate that sometimes you need to know how to get the right person involved to resolve a problem. A lot of time and effort can be wasted if the matter does not get to the appropriate person or agency. Matters sometimes have to go right to the top to get a quick and effective response.

Unsolvable Noise Complaint

Sometimes, the noise complaints are simply not solvable. I remember a noise complaint I received regarding a popular shopping mall in West Vancouver. This mall was going through a sizable expansion and was creating a lot of construction noise through the day, sometimes even late into the night and early morning. The construction noise was simply too much to bear for the nearby residents. They were against excessive noise and simply wanted the construction to stop. The West Vancouver noise by-law at that time did exempt certain conditions and sometimes would allow the construction work to go on into the night and on the weekend. The complainants would not bother to listen to the exemption and simply wanted all the construction noise to stop. The complainants did not know or care that the project had valid building permits. There was nothing much I could do; I simply had no jurisdiction to resolve noise problems of this nature. I received an earful of displeasure, sometimes abusive and obscene comments, and blame for inaction. I was so happy when the project was finally completed and no more construction noise complaints were received.

Noise caused by a wind-chime across the street?

I was sitting in my office and the telephone rang, so I answered. An apartment resident was complaining that a small ornamental wind-chime from an apartment across the street was interrupting her sleep.

When I was talking to the complainant, I was somewhat displeased and even angry. I thought this must be a very unhappy person who has to complain, not about the traffic noise, but a regular wind-chime. I suggested closing the window, which should resolve or at least reduce the wind-chime noise. The complainant's reply a big "NO" and said, "I don't want to close the window and it is my right not to." I certainly got an earful.

I had to deal with this complaint and eventually visited the apart-ment across the street where the wind-chime was located. I explained to the occupant that the noise was bothering someone across the street. Initially, this occupant was very angry and could not believe that someone across the street would complain about the pleasant sound. In the end, this occupant advised me that he was actually moving to another apart-ment in a week. I was just lucky that this noise complaint was resolved by itself. This is probably another one of God's miracles.

Garbage smell from the District of North Vancouver Landfill

I remember when the District of North Vancouver Landfill on Premier Street was in operation and numerous complaints were received from the nearby residents, especially in the hot, windy summer months.

These kinds of complaints were really difficult to deal with because there is no permanent solution. From time to time, cosmetic responses and touch and go solutions such as regular covering of the exposed garbage resulted in much displeasure between the complainants and the landfill staff.

The only permanent solution was for the resident to move out of the area or to close down the landfill, but both approaches were not feasible.

When the landfill was finally closed permanently, the garbage smell complaint was finally resolved. Following the landfill closure, the complainants' concerns were channelled to the environmental and pollution issues such as leachates into the adjacent creek. Fortunately, my inspection district was changed and I did not have to deal with the landfill area anymore, but I can understand the whole "NIMBY" not-in-my-backyard attitude. However, people create garbage. Garbage must go somewhere. Wherever garbage goes, it stinks. So what else do you expect?

Unreasonable Garbage Complaints

I remember that it was very cold and had snowed heavily for several days. A woman called and complained about her garbage that was not picked up by the municipal sanitation crew on the scheduled garbage pick-up day. It was an unusually heavy snowfall for several days and the complainant was living in an area with a very steep hill in West Vancouver. Of course, the sanitation crew was not able to get to her steep lane to pick up her garbage. This woman was blaring over the phone, yelling that nobody cared and demanded her garbage to be removed immediately. I referred the complaint to the municipal sanitation department and that was the end of it.

Another unreasonable complaint regarding garbage involved a delicatessen and catering operation situated immediately in front of a high rise apartment building separated by a back lane. At the back, this delicatessen had one big commercial garbage bin plus five or six smaller regular galvanized seventy liter household garbage containers. Several highrise tenants lived on the third and fourth floor facing the back of this delicatessen were complaining to my office regularly about the garbage situation. These tenants persistently complained about the unsightly garbage, smell and occasional over-flow of the garbage bins at the back of this delicatessen.

Every four or five days, the bins would fill, even a little too much, and the tenants would call to complain. These regular complaints carried on non-stop for at least two or three years. Every time I received the complaint, I responded by inspecting the garbage area of the delicatessen. Most of the time when I arrived I found the garbage bin was already emptied by the garbage disposal company, so the problem was resolved.

I do believe sometimes that it was partly garbage mismanagement by the delicatessen operator that caused the complaint. Because of my numerous complaint inspections made to this premise, I saw a big improvement regarding the garbage situation. I also felt that the complainants were getting to be so unreasonable, expecting the garbage area to be spic and span at all times. The complainants were not able to accept that the garbage bins are to be used every day and would be filled at a certain time and then emptied. These complainants simply wanted the garbage area clean and the garbage bins empty at all times. In the end, I was sympathetic to the operator. This operator later became a celebrity starring in a popular reality TV series.

I remember another similar unreasonable garbage complaint involving a low rental housing complex with over a hundred units in the City of North Vancouver. This low rent housing complex placed a large commercial garbage bin on a concrete pad right next to the side-walk. Several residents nearby and across this low rental complex complained consistently that the garbage was over flowing with debris on the ground.

It was also partly the mismanagement of the manager and irresponsible tenants of the housing complex. Eventually, after numerous complaints and inspections, this low rent housing complex increased the garbage pick-up frequency and built an enclosure with a lock to cover up the garbage bin. Since the enclosure was built, no garbage complaints were received because the nearby residents were not able to see if the garbage bins were full or not. No more eyesores. Again, some of these complainants would not accept that the garbage bin is to be used every day, will be full at a certain time, and would be emptied on the designated pick-up day.

Chapter 11

Weird Telephone Calls

911 Call

A woman found a hair in her restaurant meal and called 911 after trying to register a complaint with the restaurant's management. She was not satisfied with the way the management responded, so she decided to call 911 to file a complaint. The 911 operator was finally able to relay to the caller that she was tying up the emergency line, and the woman finally agreed to disconnect. She used a cell phone that did not display the phone number for tracing, or else the police department might consider laying a charge.

Prank Call to Activate the Fire Alarm

In 2011, several fast food and other restaurants in the Metro Vancouver area received phone calls in which the called claimed to be the fire department. They asked the responding staff to activate the fire alarm immediately. Many staff did without question. This caused the fire extinguishing system and the automatic sprinkling system to discharge, which contaminated all the exposed food in the kitchen.

The victimized restaurants had to discard the contaminated food in the kitchen and close down for one or two days for cleaning. Clearance from the fire and health department was required before they were allowed to reopen. Fortunately, most of the victimized restaurants were covered by their insurance for their loss. Several months after the incident, according to the local newspaper, the police were able to locate a teenager who was responsible with these prank calls.

Residential wood burning fireplace smoke complaint

I attended a health inspector annual educational conference in Richmond. It was about 3:30 PM and I was taking a break in the hotel lobby. I was checking my telephone message at the office and the following was a recording message, which my secretary was able to recapture:

"Hello Mr. Lee,

I contacted you last year in regards to a problem I've been having with a neighbour who has been burning wood in his fireplace and the fact that NOBODY [*yelling on the phone*] is addressing this MAJOR [*yelling*] environmental and health hazard problem in West Vancouver or anywhere on the North Shore. They are not addressing it – there are vulnerable people like myself who suffer from asthma and 2 distinct disabilities from which I can suffer and do suffer relapses as a result of a nearby neighbour burning wood in his open fireplace, the smoke going straight up in the air and coming into my nose. He's polluting the environment outside. Last night it was stinky with his stenchy smoke and coming into my house via my furnace when I turn on the fan. When the fan comes on and brings in so called fresh air from outside it brings his smoke... [*mumblings*] in now....plus he's polluting the outside....it's disgusting and this has been going on December, January, February and March of last year. I contacted you to do something.... NOBODY'S DOING ANYTHING [*shouting*]....nobody's taking responsibility and my health and those of the people around me in this neighborhood are being DAMAGED [*shouting*]. When

PETER K. P. LEE

are you going to be doing something about it? WHEN [*shouting*]? The only thing that has happened – I have written hundreds of letters and the GVRD... visited his house and told him the proper way to burn and this and that. There are no known laws covering, no bylaws, no laws covering his smoke.... Yes, yes he can be fined, he can be taken to court by the municipality...NOTHING HERE, NOTHING, NOTHING [*very loud shouting*]. You people aren't doing anything to protect my health and those people who are vulnerable to wood smoke and the health hazard. NOTHING ARE YOU DOING! [*loud shouting*] HOW DARE YOU! [*louder and shouting*] WE PUT YOU, WE HIRE YOU, OUR TAX PAYERS' MONEY PAYS FOR YOU AND WHAT DO YOU DO? YOU SIT ON YOUR ASSES AND DO NOTHING. Talking to these people like my neighbour who are arrogant and self-serving who have no social or moral conscience they don't care .... [*the telephone recording tape timer ran out and message stopped*]"

The same caller left a second message maybe a minute after the first one. The message is as follows:

"YOU HAVE TO DO SOMETHING ABOUT THIS PROBLEM [*yelling*] – YOU HAVE TO [*shouting*]. This is about – it's about health. YOU HAVE TO. I AM NOT TAKING NO FOR AN ANSWER ANYMORE. I AM NOT ALLOWING YOU TO PASS THE BUCK – THE BUCK STOPS WITH YOU AND YOUR DEPARTMENT AND YOUR CHIEF ENVIRONMENTAL HEALTH OFFICER. YOU HAVE TO DO SOMETHING TO PROTECT OUR HEALTH [*loud shouting*] – YOU HAVE TO [*even louder shouting*]. My name is...... telephone number.....and I am waiting. I've been waiting for a freaking year – actually the first time I called you

was 1998 about this problem and what have you done –
NOTHING [*loudest shouting*]!``

I must say that in all my years of working as a health inspector, the above messages are probably the highlight. This caller, a West Vancouver resident, claimed to have called me a year before regarding her problem. That never happened to the best of my knowledge. I did recognize the caller's name, but that was regarding the debris and cigarette butts that were in the bus-stop area.

Of course, I had to bring this complaint to my chief's attention and he decided to red-flag this caller. Further calls from this complainant would go to chief PHI, and I was so glad that I didn't have to receive this kind of call. She called the chief PHI and my medical health officer several times with the same attitude. Later I found out this caller had called several government agencies and was leaving many abusive and obscene messages like the above. The West Vancouver City Hall staff members were well aware of this caller.

The wood burning fireplace complaint simply could not be dealt with because there was no such regulation or even bylaws at the time on the North Shore. This wood burning oven smoke problem was recognized and discussed in the Greater Vancouver Regional District, but still no regulation or by-law was in place, even at the time of my retirement.

Chapter 12

Enforcement

In the 70s, it was much easier for enforcement by the health inspector. Most of the time, when the health inspector believes that there is a significant health violation, then a simple verbal order for closure was enough. In those days, the majority of the operators accepted the authority of the health inspector and do not challenge the decision, especially in the rural areas. Many ethnic restaurant operators highly respect PHIs and are even afraid of them. In fact, I do believe that a health inspector could make the life of the restaurant operators very difficult. I had heard from an ethnic restaurant operator that there are two very important persons or "Godfathers" to deal with while running the restaurant business (1) the manager of the bank and (2) the health inspector.

Enforcement gradually became more complex and not as straight forward as in the 70s. In order to properly close down a restaurant, it could still be done initially by a verbal order, but must be followed up with a proper written and signed order stating the condition that was in contravention with the health regulations. This written closure order would be posted right on the front door of the restaurant. The health inspector would re-inspect the restaurant and if the violation has been rectified then the restaurant can be re-opened.

Restaurant operators' attitudes have changed, especially in the big city situation. Restaurant operators in the big city are quite willing to challenge the closure order or the violation orders because they are more concerned with their rights. These operators would often hire a lawyer to challenge the health regulation orders. The health inspector needs to make sure the health violation order is correct and justified with no mistakes.

Maybe I was blessed or simply very fortunate that I did not have to use much enforcement authority to resolve problems or conflicts with operators. I believe if you look hard enough, that there is always a solution for every problem. To reach a compromise, it always requires mutual understanding, sincerity, and patience between the inspector and the operator.

It was my practice that if the problem does not create an immediate and serious health issue, then I am always willing to give the operator a little more time to resolve it. It is very important that the operator understands the consequence and what the ultimate action will be if they do not comply. Throughout my career, I could be friendly, respectful, and sympathetic with operators, but I was very careful not to be a real friend. I believe that it is difficult to enforce regulations with the operator once you are too friendly. It creates awkwardness because the operator will get too comfortable when you come to inspect.

I consider myself fortunate that I did not have to issue a single violation ticket, but was able to resolve health issues with all my operators. I did issue two closure orders restaurants. I issued one for four days to a Vietnamese restaurant due to serious sanitation violations. The second was issued to a sushi restaurant for ten days due to a serious cockroach infestation. I had to issue a fair number of closure orders to public swimming pools and whirl pools. Also, one time I had to condemn and dispose of a six-door walk-in-cooler filled with perishable foods such as cheese, milk, dairy products, and processed meats because it was out of operation for at least fifteen hours At the time of the inspection, the cooler reached an unsafe temperature above 21 degrees Celsius. The condemned foods were probably valued at above $10,000. All these unsafe food were properly disposed of with the assistance of my chief PHI. A couple of weeks after, I learned from this grocery operator that he had no insurance to cover this loss.

Chapter 13

Encounters with TV, Radio & Newspaper

During my career as a public health inspector, I was once filmed briefly on BCTV. I was responding to a complaint concerning some exotic birds that were kept in an industrial warehouse in North Vancouver. When I arrived at the site and was checked the area of the warehouse, I unexpectedly bumped into a TV reporter who was covering the same story. During that inspection, unfortunately, the warehouse door was locked, no attendant was found, and windows were covered. The reporter and I decided to come back at another time. That evening, my wife and I watched the news, and even though it was very short, we were amused to see me on TV.

I was also invited to the Chinese radio talk show several times regarding food safety issues and role of the health inspector. A couple of times I did live talk shows by phone without going to the station. One time, I was invited to the radio station to do a live talk show and answer questions when listeners called in. Thinking back, it was a very good experience that no words can describe. My children recorded all my talk shows and I still have the tapes today.

It was right at the beginning of my Foodsafe level one teaching class at the North Vancouver Lucas Centre when my course co-ordinator told me a newspaper reporter was coming to do an interview during my class. The reporter interviewed my co-ordinator and the camera pointed at me in front of the class during the teaching. The following week, my wife, my children, and I were amused again to see my picture and the article in *The North Shore News.*

PETER K. P. LEE

Chapter 14

Public Health Inspectors on Strike for Three Months

Sometimes, a strike can really make a person consider the value of one's occupation to society.

From early February to early May 1981, the Canadian Union of Public Employees (C.U.P.E.) was on strike. Public health inspectors in the Metro Vancouver area are CUPE members, but we were considered to be a non-essential service so we were on strike as well. During these three months, I did my union member duty by carrying the picket sign all through different work sites on the North Shore. During this time, the weather was unusually cold, particularly at night. The early picketing shifts were unbearable.

I remember that I had to picket for several early morning shifts at the North Vancouver landfill at the end of Premier Street. There were about a dozen of us CUPE members walking and blocking the entrance at the landfill. We were successful in stopping most of the commercial truckers such as those from Smithrite Disposal. Many truckers were Teamster Union members themselves and were therefore very sympathetic, so they simply turned around and left. There were other contentious situations in which non-union truckers persistently kept moving forward, ignoring the picket line. I remember that our picket captain at the landfill was a small-built woman, but was she ever feisty and determined, leading about ten of us CUPE members walking and stopping in front of the truckers that wanted to go through. What a fight we put up! Some of these actions were also captured and reported on *The North Shore News*.

I am sure that the restaurant operators in the Metro Vancouver area were very happy knowing that the health inspectors would not be coming in to check them.

One of the big concerns in the early and mid period of the strike was the garbage situation for the residents and restaurants. There were no disastrous food poisoning outbreaks, nor reporting of any communicable disease outbreaks. There was no municipal garbage removal service for the entire time and many unionized garbage disposal companies were not able to get access to the local landfill. The garbage simply accumulated in back lanes. These and other not frequently visited areas became miniature landfills.

Newspaper reporters and the public were concerned that if the garbage accumulation continued, it would be bad enough to be declared a significant health hazard. The Metro Vancouver medical health officer expressed the opinion that it was not a significant health hazard yet, and therefore no immediate action was carried out.

I believe that because it was still early spring, with such unusual cold temperatures, the risk was small that a serious communicable disease or food borne illness incident would occur. If this strike took place in the summer, it would be quite different with many more health problems. I am sure that both the management and the union did not anticipate such a long strike.

Many union members suffered extreme financial difficulty and some lost their houses because mortgage payments were not kept up. The strike pay was $50 a week, which would not go far to support a family and a mortgage. The later stage of the strike was in April, which is normally tourist time, meaning many people come to Vancouver to spend their money, particularly in restaurants. The union started an advertising and publicizing campaign, sending the message to the United States warning them that they could be at risk because the health inspectors were not inspecting the restaurants and hotels. This campaign probably contributed some pressure to the municipal management and the strike was finally over by early May 1981.

During the strike, I felt confused, especially when I was picketing at the landfill entrance. I thought my job as a health inspector was to protect the public health and ensure proper disposal of garbage. But at this time,

I was preventing the garbage from being removed. This action contradicted what I was taught and trained to do as a public health inspector.

I was very proud to be a public health inspector. I considered my work to be significant, essential, and important enough to make a positive difference in society. After the strike, I asked myself how significant my work is if I could walk away for three months without anything changing.

Chapter 15

2010 Olympic Games

Many health inspectors spend their entire career without having the opportunity to work during an Olympic Games. I considered myself fortunate to work during the 2010 Olympic Games in Vancouver. The event took place throughout different municipalities in the Lower Mainland including, Richmond, Vancouver, North Shore, and Whistler. Our office, Vancouver Coastal Health North Shore, covered the Olympic venue on Cypress Mountain. Our office was responsible for checking the water supply, sewage disposal, restaurants, and food concessions. From our office, seven health inspectors worked in teams of two to inspect Cypress Mountain daily right through the entire Games. Two other health inspectors from our office did the same coverage in Whistler.

It was exciting! I remember the process of getting the accreditation I.D., paper work, security check, and Vancouver Coastal Health Uniform. Also, the weather in 2010 was unusually warm, so there was not enough snow on the mountain for the events. To compensate for the insufficient snow, more had to be brought in to the event areas. It was memorable seeing trucks and trucks of snow from Manning Park, which is more than a hundred kilometres away, lining up on Cypress. It was unloaded by helicopter bit by bit. Because of the lack of snow, stacks of hay served as safety landing blockades for the athletes. They were transported and arranged by helicopters to form a safe landing blockade for the athletes. The ice transporting trucks, the helicopters, and the accompanying loud noises were so unforgettable. I remember seeing a group of about fifty

RCMP officers doing the trial run, skiing up and down the hill. They provided the security on Cypress Mountain. I was proud and honoured to be able to provide my services for the 2010 Olympic Games.

One memorable moment while I was on duty on Cypress Mountain was hearing the crowds roar and cheer when Canada won its first medal. Later, I learned that Jennifer Heil won a silver medal for Canada in the moguls event. The most unforgettable event was the last medal that Canada won. It was the final hockey game between Canada and the United States. In the last few moments of overtime, Sidney Crosby scored the winning goal for Canada. The cheers were heard right through the city because many Vancouverites were watching the game at home. That final score made our men's hockey team the gold medal champions. It was such an exciting game and I was so proud to be a Canadian.

The 2010 Olympics was a special event that helped me reflect on the meaning of C.P.H.I. (C), which stands for Certificate in Public Health Inspection (Canada). My identity as a certified Canadian public health inspector was strongly reinforced when I got all my special uniform gear and my I.D. for working at the different Olympic sites. Even off duty when I was walking the streets of various Olympic venues, enjoying the festive atmosphere, and the excitement of the world coming together in Vancouver, Canada for the Games, I found myself looking at the food vendors, the garbage and waste systems, portable toilets, etc. with the analytical eye of a health inspector. But the Olympics wasn't all about work, of course! Every time a Canadian stepped up on the podium to receive a medal and "O Canada" was playing, my heart was right there with them, proud that a fellow Canadian has achieved success. As a Canadian not born in Canada, the 2010 Olympic Games and my involvement with the Games as a health inspector deepened my sense of being a Canadian. I realize that participating in the Olympics as a part of my career is a rare opportunity that I never would have thought possible.

Chapter 16

Dealing with the boss

When you have a complaint and you do not know what to do, naturally you go to the boss for assistance. Many times when I did this, my headache got bigger, I became more confused, and left with no practical remedy to the situation. Often the boss does not want to get involved and does not know what to do except to simply ramble on and on to save face with no solution offered.

Even when no assistance is offered, if you resolve the complaint properly yourself, the boss will claim the glory and credit. I admired and respected one of my former bosses who, whenever I referred a problem to him and he took over, I never heard about the problem again. This boss knew his job and was willing to take responsibility.

I remember one time my superior inspector came to me with an insect and asked, "What is this?" This insect turned out to be a small cockroach. Apparently, this superior had never seen a cockroach. I wondered how this superior got the promotion and would not even know what a cockroach looks like.

Incompetent administration in the office was my main frustration. I was often frustrated dealing with office politics and the administration. Given the nature of my job, you would think that I would be more frustrated dealing with the public, but no, I got along well with almost all members of the public. I earned respect from most of my restaurant operators, and it was mutual. My operators understood my bottom line. I would not take any unnecessary action, and when I issued correction orders, the operator would attend to them as required. I was always willing to allow more time for the operator for rectifying the matters that would not posed significant health hazards. Sometimes, I believe that I was overly sympathetic, but I received much respect and appreciation from the public, the outside agencies, and other organizations.

Watch-Dog Boss

I remember it was my birthday and I went to the Lonsdale Quay food court to have a morning coffee with a co-worker. That co-worker just bought a brand new truck and wanted to show it off. While we were walking back to the office, the co-worker invited me to walk over to the parking lot where his new truck was, just a block behind the office. After admiring this beautiful new truck, we finally walked back to the office. The entire coffee break and checking out the new truck took less than thirty minutes. After I got back to my work station and before I sat down, the boss walked in and asked me to come to his office. To my surprise, the boss was watching through the window, counting the time, and was upset that I took a thirty minute coffee break. I thought a boss should have more important work to do than peeking out the window and timing employees' coffee breaks.

When I first started working on the North Shore, this same boss was also an inspector at that time. Back then, this person once took me out to New Westminster for an entire afternoon to shop for a small motor boat. At that time, I considered this person to be reasonable and friendly. We spent many long coffee breaks together. Shortly after the promotion, this person said to another health inspector during a casual meeting, "I've changed." The boss became distant and would not go for coffee like in the old days because we were in the lower ranks.

This person, through manipulation and perhaps opportunity, was eventually promoted and became a director. This director kept up the arrogant manner of I-am-the-big-boss and was eventually disliked by many other staff. Finally, one day in the office we learned the news that this director was let go. I don't remember if there was an office farewell party, but this director simply disappeared into the background. I also remember that about a year later, a co-worker and I were having morning coffee at the Starbucks across the street from the health department. The former director was also in line a couple of people behind us. The co-worker and I could not bring ourselves to even say hello. I really felt sad that this former director at one time was a good friend of mine, but now I could not even say hello.

Back-Watching Boss

It was a heavy snowfall on a work day. Vancouverites are never prepared for driving in heavy snow due to the improper winter tires and lack of driving practice in winter conditions. Some other people and I managed to make it to work, but the driving was treacherous. Once we got to the office, we stayed at our work stations doing paper work because it was simply too snowy to venture out to do inspections. Two of the four directors made it to work that day. These two directors took turns checking every half hour or so that we were all there and working. I believe a reasonable boss should consider the staff's safety and allow people to leave early when the weather is poor.

The Boss who would not support the Staff

You would think that a boss would be proud of the achievements of their subordinates and provide excellent performance reviews or financial rewards, because this would reflect well on the boss and the organization.

In the late 1980s, it was a joint effort between a municipality and the health department to hire a noise control officer (NCO), who was to deal mainly with complex noise issues with a small role as a public health inspector. This NCO was paid on the same salary scale as a public health inspector. Other noise control officers were paid at least one or two pay grades higher than PHIs. This NCO started the re-classification process for more than two years. Eventually, the re-classification application went to a labor arbitration hearing. At the end of the hearing, the decision was that the NCO would be allocated to an appropriate class and should have received the appropriate higher salary pay grade.

This NCO had to fight alone with no support from the superiors. In the end, the NCO won the favoured decision from the arbitration, but was only offered a small sum, about $500, in compensation for work performed for more than three years. Was it worth all that effort?

Good Boss

Not all bosses are unreasonable and bad. I had two excellent bosses. The first was during my two years in Alberta when I was in a brand new one-man sub-office. My senior health inspector gave me excellent guidance and trust, and I learned a lot from him. Of course, I did not abuse the trust that I received and I sought constant advice from him, because I respected him a lot. He was almost like a father figure to me, not just at work, but after work as well. He frequently invited me to have dinner with his family.

The second good boss I had was on the North Shore. This boss went through the ranks from inspector, senior inspector, and finally chief inspector. I came across many bosses who, once they got promoted, they purposely forgot what it was like when they walked and worked daily in their district. They simply changed into a higher echelon.

This boss retained the same attitude even when he became the big chief. He told me many times, "It's just a job." I remember that whenever I had a problem and went to him, he would give me sound and practical advice. Sometimes, when the problem was too complex or too big for me to handle, he would take it off my hands and deal with it himself. This same problem would never come back to me, whereas a bad boss would make my problem bigger by snowballing.

I remember one time that my young daughter was hit by a car walking home from school and ended up in the hospital for about three months. During her stay, there was complication after complication and it took a lot out of my wife and me. I guessed my worry was showing on my face when I came to work, but this good boss showed me that he cared. He was concerned and often told me, "go to the hospital to see your daughter and don't worry about work." This kind and wonderful boss earned a lot of my respect and I learned a lot from him.

I learned that the key element of a good boss should be compassion and willingness to accept responsibility.

Chapter 17

Dealing with the Public

Throughout my thirty-eight years of dealing with the public, I found that when someone called to complain, they would be mad, irate, and agitated, and would not take any negative response. I learned to first hear them out with a sympathetic ear, to show sincerity, and then offer a solution or advice. If you are very certain that you cannot offer any assistance, then you should explain to the person why you cannot help and then refer them to an appropriate agency.

Sometimes, as soon as you picked up the phone to answer, you are immediately in the hot seat with the complainant screaming, shouting, and giving you an earful of accusations that you have nothing to do with. You have to realize that we live in a very complex society with many government agencies.

The public are often not sure which government agency to call regarding their problem. When they have received a half dozen referrals and been passed back and forth between agencies, you can appreciate why callers get so angry and irritated. I often received complaints for which I am certain there is nothing more I can do, but to make a genuine gesture of concern, I would offer to meet the person to understand the matter a little deeper. By giving this extra effort, the caller is often satisfied, even though no action was taken. It is unfortunate though that our job often would not allow us to waste unnecessary time like this. The boss and the job demand more and more inspections with limited time in a day.

When I started working on the North Shore in 1975, we had one chief and six health inspectors. The population then was just under 100,000 for all 3 North Shore municipalities (City of North Vancouver, District of North Vancouver and District of West Vancouver). In 2011, we had one manager, two supervisor PHIs and 8 health inspectors. The population in 2011, for all 3 North Shore municipalities had increased to about 175,000. The population and restaurants have grown tremendously during these 36 years, but there have been no drastic increase in the number of health inspectors.

Chapter 18

Foodsafe

Foodsafe level 1 and 2 were developed in the late 1980s. These courses are specifically designed for food handlers such as restaurant operators, food store owners, and delicatessen operators. The courses were developed by a group of public health inspectors, food specialists from the B.C. Communicable Disease Control Centre, B.C. Restaurant Association and the Foodsafe Secretariat. On July 01, 2000, the Foodsafe 1 training for food premises operators in B.C. became mandatory by regulation. A written food safety and sanitation plan was also mandatory for food premises operators prior to obtaining a health permit from the health authority. Prior to opening, a new restaurant must ensure at least one staff per shift in the restaurant is Foodsafe 1 certified.

Foodsafe 1 is highly recommended for all who work in the food industry. Community colleges, school boards, and private enterprises teach Foodsafe courses. These programs are monitored very closely by health inspectors and the Foodsafe secretariat. The updating and revising of the Foodsafe courses is continuous and frequent. I considered the Foodsafe courses to be very successful and extremely beneficial for the food industry. They became recognized and sought after by a range of groups within the food industry, such as filming caterers and high school home economic teachers.

All Foodsafe instructors have to be certified by a Foodsafety Contact person in different health authorities. During the early 90s, it was very easy to be certified to become a Foodsafe instructor, but as time went on, the certification process tightened up. In the late 2000s, the courses were so popular that individuals and private enterprises were running them as a profitable business.

I was very much involved in the Foodsafe program during my career and after my retirement. One or two of my bosses prevented me from being involved in the Foodsafety Contact committee until the late 90s. I eventually became the Foodsafety Contact person on the North Shore until my retirement in 2011. For this I oversaw the Foodsafe program in my jurisdiction by monitoring, auditing, and certifying instructors. I taught Foodsafe 1 and 2 for Vancouver Community College from the time the Foodsafe program started in the late 80s. I also taught in Cantonese. Gradually, I started to teach the course at Kwantlen University, Vancouver School Board, and the North Vancouver School District. Eventually, I got into contract teaching.

It was Brian, a program co-ordinator at the Vancouver Community College, who first gave me the opportunity in the late 80s to start teaching the Foodsafe program at VCC. He was very supportive and gave encouragement often during my teaching career.

On one or two occasions, the course that I taught received some negative feedback, but Brian trusted me and sided with me all the way. I consider him to be one of my very good friends and an excellent colleague. Brian and I kept in touch even after he switched to working for Langara Community College. I have very much enjoyed the coffee meetings and conversation with Brian over the years. Several months after my retirement, Brian and I had a very nice coffee meeting at the Langara staff cafeteria. I wanted to spend more time with him now that I am retired and have more leisure time. I was shocked and saddened that several months after that meeting, the office manager at VCC advised me that Brian had passed away. He was having some stomach problems and was admitted to the hospital. He died within a week. I felt like I lost something very precious. I regretted that I couldn't even go to his funeral because I did not know. The loss of this valued friend reminded me of the fragility of life and how we can't take anything for granted. Life can change at any moment.

PETER K. P. LEE

Teaching Foodsafe was therapeutic to me and helped release stress from my job. I really felt that I was not getting enough credit or recognition in my career as a public health inspector from my superiors.

When I taught Foodsafe, I felt that I was helping the students to learn and understand food safety practices and issues. This way, students were willingly to seek my food safety knowledge by choice, not by enforcement. I believe that once the operators understand the dos and don'ts, the whys and why nots, then they will be much more willing to comply with health regulations.

Starting from the 1980s to the time of this writing, according to my records, I have taught over five hundred Foodsafe workshops and almost ten thousand students. I get a fairly good return financially by teaching Foodsafe. I added up all the earnings that I received from it and it is very rewarding. I consider it an excellent severance pay, paid in advance, and is a lot better than a promotion. I finally realized that it was God's plan for me to teach Foodsafe, which provided satisfaction, both spiritually and financially.

I want to emphasize that I was always very careful to ensure that there was no conflict between my teaching and my regular work. I taught Foodsafe only on the weekends, evenings, or on vacation days.

At my retirement, I also started teaching a new program called Marketsafe, which is specifically designed for farmers' markets and temporary food operations. I really enjoyed teaching Foodsafe and Marketsafe and I hope this will continue to be my part-time career after retirement.

At the time of my retirement, many public health inspectors or environmental health officers jumped onto the wagon and were all teaching Foodsafe courses on a part-time basis. A few actually turned Foodsafe teaching into a family business while working full time as a PHI / EHO.

Chapter 19

Gift or Bribe from the operators?

An Italian Christmas Cake

I remember receiving my first gift two or three years after I started working on the North Shore. It was Christmas time and after inspecting an Italian food imports warehouse, the operator gave me an Italian Christmas cake, which I brought back to the office. My chief PHI wanted me to share it with all the staff. My chief later sent an official letter thanking the operator. So, I don't believe that I was taking bribe.

A stack of $20 bills was handed to me

I was just finishing an inspection of a small sandwich delicatessen and was ready to leave when the Korean operator pulled out a small stack of $20 bills. He handed me two or three hundred dollars. The delicatessen was well-maintained at the inspection and I found no obvious violations or health problem. I don't know why the operator offered me that money. Of course, I did not take it, but I thanked him and told him that there is no need for such action.

Dinner invitation from a wealthy doctor

At work during a meeting, I came across a very friendly, retired Filipino doctor who later invited me and my wife to her home for dinner. This former doctor was not operating or connected to a food premise at that time and I did not feel that there was any work conflict by accepting the invitation.

When my wife and I arrived, we saw that her luxury home was very nice. I forget what the dinner consisted of, I remember the constant attention and service of the house servants. At her home, there were at least six or seven servants cooking and serving dinner. This was in the late 1970s and I don't know many friends who had servants in the house. It was an excellent dinner and interesting conversation.

Was that dinner invitation a bribe or a perk of the job? I never really knew why it was extended but we certainly felt honored. Maybe the retired doctor really wanted to be on good terms with me in case she required a favor that may help a future business venture. We had no more contact after that dinner.

Gift as sincere appreciation from the operators?

Situations regarding gifts from the operator are difficult. I firmly believe that most of the time, they simply appreciated my working relationship with them and wanted to give a token back.

Because of the potential for bribery, I chose to minimize eating out at North Shore restaurants as much as possible. It is always my intention to pay for the meal or give an excessive tip to cover the cost. The few times that my family and I ate out at the North Shore restaurants, when coming to pay for the meal, the back and forth about payment was very embarrassing.

To accept the sincere appreciation of the operators, sometimes I would accept a cup of coffee, a small package of sampling candies, or desserts while meeting with them before or after the inspection. Once, I also accepted a $10 coffee gift card after presenting a lecture on food safety for a non-charitable organization. Many company policies allow employees to receive a small gift if its value is less than a meal, or $25.

Chapter 20

Changes to the Public Health Inspector's role since the early 1970s

Designation Change

When I graduated and completed the field training from the public health program at BCIT in 1973, I received a Certificate in Public Health Inspection (Canada). I could use the designation C.P.H.I. (C) after my name and my certificate number was 2205. In the 70s, the majority of public health inspectors working in Canada were certified with C.P.H.I. (C) except in the eastern provinces. As time went on, all public health inspectors working in Canada required a C.P.H.I. (C).

While working in Alberta, I came across quite a few older public health inspectors who preferred to be called 'sanitarian' instead. Those older inspectors had a Certificate in Sanitary Inspection Canada C.S.I. (C). The Canadian Institute of Public Health Inspectors was incorporated in 1934, but was originally called Canadian Institute of Sanitary Inspectors. I prefer to be identified as a public health inspector.

In the late 80s and early 90s, the public health inspectors dealt with and enforced many issues involving noise, air, water and sewage pollution. The name 'Environmental Health Officer' came along to replace public health inspector: E.H.O instead of P.H.I. I personally insist on being identified as a public health inspector whenever required.

Education Change

When I took the Environmental Health, Public Health program at BCIT, it was a two-year program plus three months of field training. The course and field training were very good and straightforward. The oral board exam was a frightening and dreaded experience.

This exam was about an hour long and consisted of a panel of three members: a medical health officer, a chief public health inspector, and a public health engineer. The panel members would shoot questions to the candidate at will. We understood that even if we fulfilled the school courses and the field training successfully, if we failed the oral exam, we would not get the Certificate in Public Health Inspection (Canada). It was a lot of pressure on the student going into the exam. In my year, at least one student froze and could not respond under pressure. This student had to redo the oral board exam the following year.

I was told by my senior public health inspector that he received his C.P.H.I.(C) by a correspondence course. The old timers also told me that after World War II, any returning soldiers who were medics during the war easily became a sanitarian. In the 70s there were three institutions in Canada giving training for this job. One at Saint Hyacinth, Quebec, one at Ryerson Polytechnic Institute in Toronto, Ontario, and one at the British Columbia Institute of Technology, Burnaby, B.C. In the late 90s, both BCIT and Ryerson were offering a degree program for public health inspection. In the 70s, high school graduates with academic science programs were required to be accepted into the public health program at the B.C. I.T. and Ryerson. In the 90s, a bachelor's degree in science became the pre-requisite for admission into the program.

Organizational Change

In the 70s, public health inspectors could work for the three levels of government in Canada: municipal, provincial, and federal. In the 90s, many municipal public health inspectors were absorbed into the provincial systems. When I first worked in 1973 for the Sturgeon Health Unit in Redwater, Alberta, it was a provincial health unit. In 1975, I came back to B.C. and worked on the North Shore Union Board of Health, which had jurisdiction for three municipalities, the City of North Vancouver, District of North Vancouver, and District of West Vancouver. The North Shore Union Board of Health later changed its name to North Shore Health, North Shore Health Region, then Vancouver Coastal Health, and ended up becoming a provincial system. In 1975 in B.C., there were eighteen provincial health units, then fifty-two health regions and finally, by the 90s, five health authorities. The line of command in the 70s went from public health inspector, senior (supervisor) public health inspector, and deputy public health inspector to chief public health inspector. In the 90s, the line of command was changed to environmental health officer / public health inspector (EHO/PHI), senior (or supervisor) EHO/PHI, manager, deputy director, to director.

From Shirt & Tie to Uniform & Badge

When I started working as a public health inspector in the 70s, a shirt and tie were commonly accepted, but definitely no jeans or T-shirts. Some health departments even made it mandatory to wear a tie while on duty. In the 90s, golf shirts and more casual wear were considered acceptable. Jeans and casual wear were always common for the public health inspectors dealing with the sewage systems and sub-divisions. I remember that one of our PHI practicum students ran into problems because of the casual T-shirt and jeans attitude. The barber shop operator would not allow him to carry out the inspection because he did not trust that such a casually dressed young Asian fellow could be the authoritative public health inspector he expected. For quite a few years prior to my retirement, when inspecting a public school, public carnival, temporary food booth, or responding to a fire or police incident, I frequently wore a health inspector jacket and vest, and carried an I.D. badge.

Operational and Enforcement Change

During my training at BCIT, education was our first aim and working on approaches to deal with restaurant operators and the enforcement, such as a closure order, was the ultimate step. I remember one time, a medical health officer came as a guest speaker and said, "If you have to take an operator to court, then you have already failed in your job. Have you tried hard enough to communicate with or educate the operator?" I followed this philosophy right through my entire career until my retirement and it really worked well for my restaurant operators and me. I applied this philosophy and resolved many challenges. I found the majority of the public would co-operate with you as long as you are sincere and lived up to your credibility and integrity. In my entire career, I issued only two closure orders for restaurants, one due to poor sanitation and one due to heavy infestation of cockroaches. I have never issued a violation ticket.

I was very surprised two years after my retirement that quite a few former restaurant operators that I had worked with contacted me for advice dealing with their health violations or operating issues. I felt very touched because they still trust and respect my advice even after my retirement.

In the 90s, EHO / PHI members commonly wore their uniform and wrote violation tickets to the restaurant operators. It appeared some EHOs / PHIs were bragging to their colleagues about how many violation tickets or closure orders they issued. I was so glad that there was no violation ticket quota required for each health inspector to produce or I would have been forced to write tickets. Also, like I mentioned earlier in the memoir, there are the good, the bad and the ugly in all professions.

Violation ticket fines range from $200 to $500. Restaurant operators have to sell a lot of food to earn that back. The global economy in the 90s was not good and it was not so easy to be in business, particularly for restaurants. It is very competitive and the profit margins decrease with time. It was common to see restaurants change hands or close down frequently. I have seen quite a few new restaurants that were folded even before the grand opening due to the lack of funds and poor cash flow.

I could see the role of an EHO / PHI change from an educator to an enforcement officer like the police without a gun. This confirmed that it was the right timing for me to retire.

I am not putting down the ticketing system and I believe it may be necessary to deal with some stubborn operators who will not co-operate. I believe that these types of operators, a minority in my opinion, should not be in business and deserve violation tickets or even a closure order.

In my long career as a PHI, I came to the conclusion that there is no such thing as a perfect food premises or restaurant. If I really wanted to, I could always find something wrong in either facility sanitation or staff hygiene.

The ticketing system could be open to abuse by the public health inspector or environmental health officer. An inspector could purposely visit a specific restaurant at his or her own will, necessary or not, because the inspector is paid by a fixed salary for so many hours a day. The more number of inspections made to the restaurant, the more opportunity to find things wrong and issue violation tickets.

Most restaurant operators would simply pay the fine rather than fight the ticket in court. Fighting a violation ticket is time consuming and will probably cost much more financially at the end, even if you win.

Chapter 21

How to tell if a restaurant is clean and sanitary or not?

Clean Restaurant?

As a customer, how do you know the restaurant that you are about to dine in is clean? The public areas such as the lounge, dining room, and the washrooms are more visible for the diner to check out. Sometimes, even though all the accessible and public areas appear to be clean, the kitchen could be filthy. Even a very high-class restaurant could have a dirty kitchen with poor food handling procedures.

Many restaurant operators are aware that if their restaurants appear to be dirty, it will turn customers away and be bad for business. Therefore, many operators will try hard to keep the public areas in decent condition. Because the kitchen area is normally not accessible to the customer, some operators will try to cut costs by downplaying cleaning in the kitchen.

As a restaurant patron, the cleanliness of the kitchen should be paramount because if it is not clean, the food will likely be contaminated, causing foodborne illness after consumption. To prevent this, cleanliness of the premises, proper cleaning and sanitation of the utensils, and safe food handling procedures are most important.

In my experience, before you decide to dine in an unfamiliar restaurant, you should first check the washrooms. If the washroom is clean and tidy, then the restaurant is very likely fine to dine in. If the restaurant operator is willing to maintain the washroom, it suggests a clean kitchen as well. I must caution you that I have seen a very high-class restaurant in which the washroom was very messy because one bad customer went in and decided to make a mess inside. This would not be a decisive reflection of a restaurant.

You should also check to see if the restaurant is busy or not. Generally, if the restaurant is busy at dinner time, then you could assume it will serve fresh and good food because of the high turnover rate of the food. If the restaurant is not too busy, then the food served may not be very fresh. Of course, sometimes there could be a valid reason why that restaurant is not very busy that day. For example, road construction or traffic re-direction outside the restaurant could cause them to have fewer customers.

If I just want clean, safe food and am not too concerned about gourmet cooking, I would choose to eat at any one of the popular fast-food restaurant chains because they have a higher company standard. According to my career experience, I find that in general, the majority of these popular restaurant chains receive a better health inspection report.

Sanitation Rating System for restaurant by the local health department?

At the time of my retirement, health authorities in the Metro Vancouver area post on their websites all the restaurants that were ordered closed or seriously in contravention with health regulations. A restaurant-goer could check the health authority websites prior to eating in a specific restaurant.

The Toronto Health Department places restaurant sanitation in three categories: (1) Pass (2) Conditional Pass & (3) Closed. At the end of each health inspection, the inspector will give the restaurant one of the three signs according to its merit: a green sign marked PASS, a yellow sign marked CONDITIONAL PASS, or a red sign marked CLOSED. These signs are to be posted in a conspicuous area such as the front door or the front window.

I feel this system would be more effective for the consumer. The disadvantage is that it may not work well with the less experienced health inspectors because inspections involve a complex system of assessment for the entire restaurant operation.

The violation posting system is not as effective for the consumer because when you are hungry, you will find some restaurant close by to eat and you will likely not go into the website to check it out. The advantage is that it's more accurate by showing which health violation that the restaurant actually committed.

This restaurant makes tasty food?

Sometimes, if customers pay a high price, they automatically expect good, tasty food in return. I found that this is not always true. In fact, I found some very small, unnoticeable, and inexpensive restaurants that make very tasty food. Of course, the expensive restaurant will likely give you a very pleasant atmosphere and excellent service.

I remember while working in the Lower Lonsdale area during the late 1970s, there was one small and old Japanese restaurant with no visual attraction for customers that only opened for lunch. It was very busy every day with a line-up outside because the food was very tasty and had good money value. Four dollars or less would buy you a good lunch, including a small kettle of Japanese tea, a bowl of miso soup, and a good portion of the main entre such as chicken, pork, or beef with stir fried vegetables and rice.

Because business was so good, every winter, the owner would take a month off for holidays. When he returned, he was refreshed with a good sun tan.

What food to eat when you are travelling in an unfamiliar place?

My wife and I did quite a bit of travelling during our 30s and 40s and we never got sick because of the food we ate. I remember in 1991, my wife and I joined a Holy Land tour to Israel, and it was a wonderful trip. We had a very experienced pastor as our guide.

Our first stop was Tel Aviv. We had a little free time in the afternoon and strolled around the beautiful port area. A couple in our tour group decided to sample the different foods from the street vendors, and that evening both of them had very bad stomach cramps and severe diarrhea. They were better in the morning. Certainly, it is not a pleasant experience to get food poisoned while travelling.

When you are travelling in an unfamiliar place, you can avoid getting a foodborne illness by choosing what to eat very carefully. The following are some of my suggestions:

- Avoid eating food from street vendors. They often don't have adequate refrigeration and may lack clean running water, which can contribute to unsafe food.

- When you are on the road, if you are hungry and must eat something, choose food that was cooked at a high temperature —boiled, baked, or deep-fried. These will have a much smaller health risk. Liquids that have been boiled, such as hot coffee, hot tea, hot chocolate, and hot soup should be safe.

- If you do need to eat food from the street vendors you should look for their clean clothing and good hygiene practices. Street vendors with clean clothing and good hygiene such as short clean nails and clean hair will likely produce safer food.

- Avoid eating cut fruits and raw salads on the roadside because of the higher chance of contamination by insects and by poor hygiene, such as dirty hands. Whole fruit with a thick peel or rind such as bananas, and citrus fruit like oranges and grapefruit are safer to eat than thin-skinned fruit like fresh berries, grapes, or plums.

- Fresh fruit with thin skin should be washed in your hotel room with hot water and the skin peeled prior eating to minimize surface contamination because the fruit peel is often handled by dirty hands; therefore, they are likely to be contaminated with pathogens that can make you sick.

- Avoid eating food prepared in heavily fly infested areas—flies spread pathogens.

PETER K. P. LEE

- Cold food should be cold and hot food should be hot to touch. Perishable food such as meat, fish, and dairy stored at room temperature for a long period can be dangerous. If you don't know how long the food has been at room temperature, avoid it.

- Beware of bottled water sold by street vendors, especially if there is no seal or the seal is damaged or broken. These bottled water containers may have been simply filled with ordinary local tap water. These are likely recycled water bottles that may appear clean, but often are not disinfected and the liquid within might also be unsafe.

- Be aware that consuming raw foods and raw seafood, particularly shellfish, can increase your likelihood of becoming ill.

Note that the above suggestions are dependent on the environmental health conditions of the places you are travelling to. For example, in tropical climates, perishable food items like fish, meat, and dairy products will have a shorter shelf life compared to cooler climates. Also, different places have different drinking water sources that may have different degrees of safety. Even if water comes from a tap, it may not be safe due to inadequate water disinfecting systems.

When my wife and I were travelling, we always brought along a few chocolate bars, beef jerky, trail-mix (pre-packaged assorted nuts, seeds, and dried fruit), and safe bottled water. The chocolate bars and beef jerky gave us quick energy until we get back to the hotel or some restaurant that is safer to dine in. Most of the hotel continental breakfasts usually provide hard-boiled eggs. Bring a few clean sandwich bags to take away a couple of eggs, or some non-perishable items such as a croissant, non-cream and non-meat filled pastries, or cookies at the end of your breakfast before leaving your hotel. The hard-boiled eggs may not smell nice but will provide a good source of temporary energy.

Chapter 22

Family life and my career

By character, I believe that I am a very private, quiet, and somewhat shy person. I have worked in rural health units like Redwater, and in a big metropolitan area like Vancouver's North Shore. When I was working in the rural area, I often drove long distances between small hamlets and villages, with little contact with operators during the day. At the end of the day, I felt tired physically, but I was willing to do more social activities.

It was quite a difference when I worked in a big city. Every day I walked in and out, restaurant after restaurant, with problems and confrontations, and so much contact with people.

When I got home, I simply didn't want any more conversation, to see any more unnecessary faces, or take part in any social activities. Often after work, I went to my room by myself to read the newspaper or watch the news or a movie. It was difficult for my wife and my children to understand. Why the grouchy mood, and why was I so hard to please at times?

It was the nature of my job to always look for mistakes and wrong doing, and I often remained in that critical mode with my family when I got home.

Friends and co-workers may see me as gentle-mannered and soft spoken most of the time, but inside, I can be explosive and quick tempered at times, especially when I feel like I am being bluffed or taken advantage of.

I considered myself blessed with a wonderful family; a wife, daughter, and son. At the time of this writing, my wife and I have been married for thirty-eight years. My wife worked in a bank prior to our marriage. We were blessed with a daughter and a son after our marriage. We both believed it is important to do our best to bring up our children the Christian way. I consider myself fortunate that my wife was able and willing to be a home-maker while our children were growing up, from kindergarten to university. Both of our children did very well academically, right from high school to university.

I always appreciated my wife's laborious effort with many prayers to teach our children while growing up. Child psychologists say it is very important to teach children from ages one to six. You will miss the boat if the child is not brought up correctly during the first six years of his or her early life.

My daughter and son both received numerous scholarships, which covered most of their university education. They took on part-time jobs right through their high school years. They both also volunteered in non-profit organizations and served actively in the church. My daughter completed her Bachelor of Arts, Master of Arts, Bachelor of Education degrees at the University of British Columbia. My son completed both his Bachelor's and Master's Degrees in Applied Science in Computer Engineering at the University of British Columbia as well. My wife and I did not have a university education, but we are glad and proud that our children did. My daughter chose a career as a teacher. She has taught high school in both private and public schools and is currently teaching in adult continuing education. My son has chosen a career in the software industry.

PETER K. P. LEE

Chapter 23

The kind of day-to-day telephone
inquiries and complaints that I had to
deal with during the year of 1986

What kind of day-to-day telephone inquiries and
complaints that I had to deal with in 1986?

Here is a sample that shows some of my routine daily dealings with the public. I picked 1986 mainly because it was EXPO 86 in Vancouver and I had a lot of memorable and happy experiences during this event. My family had a wonderful time as well. Each of my family members had a pass, which gave us unlimited visits. My two young children particularly enjoyed the entire Exposition. The only drawback was we had to entertain many out-of-town guests; it was almost like a revolving door at our home as guest after guest came and went.

From January 1 to December 31, 1986, I had a total of 829 telephone calls from the public dealing with various enquires and complaints. It was a health department policy that a health inspector normally needs to deal with the public complaint first over the routine daily inspection. Below, I have picked the highlights:

Call #1	a woman purchased a can of beans with pork from a local store and observed bubbles in the can
Call #3	a bottled of baby food purchased from a local pharmacy store appeared to have gone bad
Call #9	a telephone consultation with the Federal Health Protection branch food inspector regarding the dented canned food products offer sale at a local store
Call #25	complaint regarding a cocoon found inside a package of toasted cracker
Call #33	complaint regarding a bad smell in the women's steam and shower- room at a local fitness club
Call #41	a woman enquires about how to bury a dead dog
Call #42	suspected food poisoning after eating at a popular fast-food restaurant
Call #43	suspected food poisoning after eating a meat pie at a popular local deli
Call #59	complaint regarding air pollution from the North Vancouver Seabus Terminal
Call #67	restaurant operator complained about garbage from their neighbour
Call #74	saw a rat in a restaurant
Call #78	a woman requested we test the water collected from the cliff run off

PETER K. P. LEE

Call #92	inquiry regarding sauna temperature
Call #99	chemical used in a business involving methanol and hydrogen
Call #114	a referral call from a medical doctor regarding his patient infected with amoebiasis
Call #147	a daughter called regarding a smell that bothers her mother who Is living in a senior care home
Call #148	a woman called regarding rust in her tap water
Call #150	mould infestation in a home
Call #160	hot water tank and related devices
Call #164	sand box for cat droppings, construction, and information
Call #180	type of garbage container for a commercial market complex
Call #192	school board staff wanted to know different methods of disinfection
Call #197	draft beer requirement for a restaurant
Call #198	a woman complained about the smelly cupboard in her apartment
Call #218	complaint about a bakery staff worker picking up baked goods with bare hands; no tongs or gloves were used
Call #250	pigeon problem under the building canopy
Call #262	inquiry regarding Purichlor (a new pool water disinfection device)

Call #265   septic tank system for a private home

Call #279   customer complained that he was not able to get a new coffee
                 cup for refill

Call #290   stale and outdated package of nachos found in a local store

Call #293   female apartment tenant wanted to know if a sand box presents
                 a health hazard

Call #296   an apartment shared by three tenants. One of them was
                 complaining about the filthy condition of their shared washroom

Call #297   tenant complained that the apartment hallway was not
                 vacuumed

Call #300   complaint of the dirty and messy condition of his co-tenant.

Call #313   a woman called regarding flat lacquer vapour

Call #329   health requirement for a camp changing / shower room

Call #365   a bakery staff member picked up baked goods and handled
                 money with bare hands at the same time.

Call #367   do preservative chemicals used at the Lonsdale Quay dock
                 present a health hazard?

Call #371   poor hygiene of the food handling staff

Call #388   Fire incident notification and request for health inspection from
                 the City of North Vancouver Fire Department

Call #394   complaint that users were not taking a shower before going into
                 the pool at the North Vancouver Recreation Centre.

Call #397	women enter the swimming pool without cleansing shower after the aerobics exercise class on the pool deck
Call #398	air-gap requirement for a swim pool.
Call #413	anonymous complaint of bad odor from a seafood restaurant.
Call #422	referral from the City of North Vancouver City Hall regarding a chemical spray used at a local gas station.
Call #424	complaint involved sandblasting of outside walls of a building
Call #440	health inspection request regarding sewage back up
Call #446	apartment dweller called regarding blue stains from tap water
Call #450	rat sighting
Call #451	report of a cat in a swimming pool
Call #452	percolation test inquiry
Call # 464	no heat in the apartment.
Call #474	garbage complaint in the area where she lives
Call #479	requesting information for cleaning and disinfecting after flooding for her house
Call #490	bug in the Deep Cove water supply
Call #501	suspect food poisoning after eating shrimp purchased from a popular food store in Lynn Valley
Call #504	barking dog complaint from an irate citizen

Call #505	contracting eye infection after swimming in the pool
Call #513	garbage in the back lane
Call #519	brown sugar purchased from a food warehouse tasted soapy
Call #529	wading pool requirement inquiry
Call #532	high mineral content in the water supply
Call #546	hearing dog allowed in the restaurant
Call #547	public health nurse inquired about what chemical to use for treating fleas
Call #548	garbage from a restaurant
Call #552	suspected foodborne illness after eating a chicken burger sandwich at a popular fast food restaurant in Vancouver
Call #554	garbage complaint in the lane behind commercial premises
Call #558	sun-tanning device
Call #568	brown particles in the water supply
Call #564	exotic bird in the residential area
Call #567	referral from a hospital social worker concerning a patient living in a filthy apartment
Call #572	noise complaint against a commercial garbage truck picking up garbage too early in the morning
Call #573	what pesticide to use for gnats

PETER K. P. LEE

Call #578	referral from City Hall regarding restaurant garbage
Call #595	unsanitary coffee cup handling by a restaurant staff
Call #599	worms found inside cod filet purchased from a local fish market
Call #604	anonymous complaint for picking up lice from a shopping mall pubic washroom
Call #612	suspected foodborne illness after eating at a popular restaurant in Stanley Park area
Call #635	staff with a big bandage on her palm handled food.
Call #637	magic mushrooms growing in the yard of her house and a teenager was picking them
Call #652	a physician called regarding toxic fumes from a dry cleaning operation
Call #657	consultation with the federal product safety inspector regarding the safety of a popular children's toy
Call #663	ICBC staff called regarding cleaning and disinfecting of the hand-sets and telephones
Cal #664,	garbage left in the lane
Call #669	water leakage problem in a strata condominium
Call #675	a popular brand of milk tasted like oil
Cal #577	neighbour threw kitty litter into her lawn
Call #685	suspected foodborne illness after eating at a coffee shop

Call #689   commercial awning requirement

Call #692   anonymous caller sighting a cat in the store; also mouldy bread

Call #695   tap water smells like bleach

Call #698   resident called regarding no water supply in Deep Cove

Call #708   level of fluoride in the water supply

Call #718   consultation with the health protection branch regarding the banning of the popular Gold Coin Chocolate

Call #721   suspect foodborne illness after eating at a popular fast food restaurant

Call #723   garbage problem at a popular local store

Call #727   referral from City of North Vancouver staff regarding garbage inside the CNR rail tunnel

Call #729   milk sampling inquiry

Call #733   tap water appeared dirty in the Capilano Road area

Call #746   animal control request

Call #760   woman called regarding worms found inside the honey tangerine orange purchased from a local produce store

Call #762   suspect food poisoning after eating chilli from a local deli

Call #765   complaint regarding no garbage pick-up

Call #767   bugs in her kitchen cupboard

Call #769   asbestos tape and health hazards

Call #770   sighting of a mouse in a popular local restaurant

Cal #771,   anonymous caller complaining a bag of smelly fish in the lane

Call #772   consultation with plumbing inspector regarding lead content inside hot water tank

Call #785   a father called and suspected his daughter picked up a vaginal infection after using the municipal pool

Cal #794,   a dentist called and inquired about the fluoride concentration of the water supply

Call #814   a Burnaby resident called regarding a yellow cloud overhanging a chemical refinery in North Vancouver area

Call #820   a woman complained that a garbage container lid is not being closed

Chapter 24

The kind of day-to-day telephone inquiries and complaints that I had to deal with during the last 9 months prior to my retirement in 2011

What kind of day-to-day telephone inquiries and complaints that I had to deal with in 2011 compared to 25 years ago in 1986

At the time of my retirement, the kind of day-to-day inquiries and complaints were extended to different areas because of the additional regulations from the Tobacco Control Act, trans fat regulation, Foodsafe, and Marketsafe.

In 2011 I worked my final year working as a public health inspector before my retirement. That year I worked nine full months from January to the end of September and had a total of 621 telephone calls or inquiries.

You could see the routine suspected foodborne illness and garbage complaints seemed to be the same as twenty-five years before. Environmental issues such as air quality and noise, and increasing pest problems such as rodents and bed bugs added to my work, along with the Foodsafe Program and the trans fat regulation.

Call #10   Foodsafe certificate information inquiry

Call #11	Foodsafe certificate replacement request
Call # 14	nail spa inspection request
Call # 15	proposed mobile catering
Call # 20	Foodsafe exam request
Call # 21	Foodsafe certificate information inquiry
Call # 22	complaint of a restaurant chef feeding the crows outside
Call # 24	air quality complaint
Call # 26	community centre water fountain circulation / filtration concern
Call # 27	sewage back up incident at a bakery
Call #31	proposed nail spa
Call # 32	complaint referral received from Canadian Food Inspection Agency (CFIA) against a butcher shop
Cal # 34,	trans fat regulation inquiry
Call # 35	Foodsafe information request
Call # 36	complaint regarding no sneeze guard at a sushi bar
Call # 40	proposed total body care operation
Call # 42	Foodsafe information request
Call # 44	trans fat regulation inquiry

PETER K. P. LEE

Call # 45   tenant with bed bug problem

Call # 48   Foodsafe information inquiry

Call # 49   Foodsafe information inquiry

Call # 50   veins and fat inside a chub of lean-hamburger meat

Call # 52   Foodsafe information request

Call # 53   trans fat regulation inquiry

Call # 55   horseradish sauce used by a popular fast food restaurant is potentially hazardous food

Call # 64   trans fat regulation inquiry

Call # 65   questioning the safety of an eye tinting chemical compound used in the beauty salon

Call # 66   suspected foodborne illness six hours after eating a fish-burger from a local fast food restaurant

Call # 72   Foodsafe information inquiry

Call # 73   bed bug information inquiry

Call # 74   Foodsafe information inquiry

Call # 77   safe food practice at a care home?

Call # 83   proposed massaging operation

Call # 85   hand sink requirement at a personal service

Call # 93	suspected foodborne illness after eating at a restaurant and was poorly treated when reported to the restaurant
Call # 94	farmers market health approval request
Call # 99	Foodsafe information request
Call # 100	low-temperature dish washer information inquiry
Call # 101	pool permit fee and invoice
Call # 102	food safety plan inquiry
Call # 103	follow up on prank fire calls to several popular local restaurants
Call # 107	Foodsafe information inquiry
Call # 108	Foodsafe certificate replacement request
Call # 113	Foodsafe information inquiry
Call # 117	mould growth on windows
Call # 121	pool permit invoice
Call # 123	Foodsafe certificate replacement request
Call # 126	Foodsafe information inquiry
Call # 132	Foodsafe instructor application inquiry
Cal # 134,	mice and hording problem of her mother living in her own home
Call # 139	suspected foodborne illness after eating a donair at a pizza place

Call # 143   tobacco smoking complaint

Call # 150   Foodsafe exam request

Call # 152   tobacco smoking complaint

Call # 156   rash developed after swimming in an aquatic centre

Call #163   freon gas leak from the freezer of a local supermarket bakery department

Call # 167   low-temperature dishwasher information

Call # 170   proposed wood burning of a mobile pizza trailer

Call # 179   a bug found in food at a popular local Chinese restaurant

Call # 183   tobacco smoking complaint

Call # 184   safe drinking water quality inquiry

Call # 186   strong chlorine odour from the tap water

Call # 192   proposed nail spa

Call # 193   smoking in patio area

Call # 198   health requirement for serving coffee at a pet shop

Cal # 204,   tobacco smoking room

Call # 205   patio seating smoking complaint

Call # 206   new swim pool regulation inquiry

Call # 211   Foodsafe certificate replacement request

Call # 212   health requirement for a potluck dinner at a local school

Call # 234   use of butter vs. margarine

Call # 236   suspected foodborne illness after eating a taco at a local restaurant

Call # 238   proposed beauty salon and health requirement

Call # 241   Foodsafe instructor application and information inquiry

Call # 243   outstanding pool permit fee and collection

Call # 247   outstanding restaurant permit fee and collection

Call # 264   Foodsafe information inquiry

Call # 265   Foodsafe information inquiry

Call # 266   suspected foodborne illness after eating at a local hamburger restaurant

Call # 268   proposed spa inquiry

Call # 270   Foodsafe information inquiry

Call # 272   proposed chiropractor clinic and health approval

Call # 274   untidy vacant property

Call # 279   a wild cat in the residential area attacking her domestic cat

Call # 284   mould in commercial manufactured jar of antipasto

Call # 287	milk purchased from a local chain supermarket tasted off
Call # 289	outdoor pool information vs. new pool regulation inquiry
Call # 290	outdoor pool information vs. new pool regulation inquiry
Call # 291	irate public complained that the milk purchased has curdled
Call # 295	Foodsafe information request
Call # 296	proposed vending machine commissary and health requirement
Cal # 297,	new pool regulation information request
Call # 298	new pool regulation information request
Call # 299	permit fee refund request
Call # 300	swimming & whirl pool vs. new pool regulation inquiry
Call # 301	Foodsafe information inquiry
Call # 302	lab result of the mouldy antipasto
Call # 304	temporary food booth (TFB) application
Call # 305	suspected foodborne illness from eating at a Vietnamese restaurant
Call # 308	mould and indoor air quality information
Call # 309	pool flow meter information inquiry
Call # 310	outdoor pool vs. new pool regulation inquiry

Call # 311   complaint regarding sandbox in public parks

Call #312   sandbox requirement in public parks

Call # 313   sandbox health requirement in public parks

Call # 317   dirty washroom at a local sub sandwich shop

Call # 318   new pool regulation inquiry

Call # 319   moisture damage and dampness of the caller's apartment

Call # 320   new pool regulation vs. outdoor swim pool

Cal # 321,   Foodsafe instructor application request

Cal # 326,   suspected foodborne illness after eating a pepperoni mushroom pizza from a popular pizza premise

Call # 331   Foodsafe certificate replacement request

Call # 333   pool flow meter information inquiry

Call # 332   complaint regarding no sign posting of showering before entering the pool

Call # 335   Foodsafe certificate replacement request

Call # 336   suspected foodborne illness after eating at a sushi restaurant

Call # 341   Foodsafe certificate replacement request

Call # 348   health permit fee and collection

Call # 349   health permit fee and collection

Call # 350   hand sink requirement for a spa

Call # 353   recycling foods at a local pancake restaurant

Call # 356   mould and excessive moisture in a rental apartment

Call # 317   outdoor pool and the new pool regulation

Call # 358   air filters in the building not being changed

Call # 363   trans fat regulation inquiry

Call # 365   temporary food booth application

Call # 367   Foodsafe certificate request

Call # 371   private water system approval inquiry

Call # 374   setting up a Reiki operation at a basement home and health
                 requirement

Call # 383   water sampling request

Call # 385   Foodsafe certificate replacement request

Call # 395   Foodsafe certificate replacement request

Call # 396   day-care inspection requested

Call # 397   West Vancouver smoking by-law information inquiry

Call # 398   Foodsafe certificate replacement request

Call # 399   Foodsafe certificate replacement request

Call # 402   complaint regarding outdated milk purchased from a grocery

Call # 404   proposed electrolysis operation and health requirement

Call # 408   Foodsafe information inquiry

Call # 409   complaint regarding a tenant with a mental problem

Call # 410   Foodsafe certificate replacement request

Call # 411   Foodsafe certificate replacement request

Call # 412   health permit fee refund request

Call # 413   complaint regarding a strata owner with hoarding and mental problem

Call # 414   private water system information and inquiry

Call # 419   suspected foodborne illness after eating cooked oysters at a local restaurant

Call # 421   Foodsafe certificate replacement request

Call # 424   noise and tobacco smoking in the patio seating complaint against a coffee shop

Call # 435   temporary food booth application request

Call # 439   Foodsafe certificate replacement request

Call # 440   temporary food booth application request

Call # 450   Foodsafe certificate information inquiry

Call # 452 tobacco smoking complaint

Call # 455 Foodsafe certificate information inquiry

Call # 456 requirement of the new swim pool deck?

Call # 458. night market application and inquiry

Call # 462 swimming pool water sampling request

Call # 464 Foodsafe information inquiry

Call # 470 complaint regarding tobacco smoking in a municipal community garden

Call # 471 suspect foodborne illness after eating pizza at a popular local pizza restaurant

Call # 473 Foodsafe certificate replacement request

Call # 475 commercial glass-washer, sanitizer and its concentration

Call # 476 nail spa has no hand sink

Call # 477 temporary food booth application request

Call # 478 outdoor seating and health requirement inquiry

Call # 479 farmer's market and health requirement

Call # 485 garbage pick-up at 4 AM and making too much noise

Call # 486 farmer's market information inquiry

Call # 488 commercial garbage pick-up too early at 4 AM & noise problem

Call # 489	emergency generator testing notification & noise concern
Call # 490	health requirement for setting up a floatation tank operation
Call # 493	trans fat regulation inquiry
Call # 494	noise complaint
Call # 498	suspect foodborne illness after eating sushi
Call # 500	complaint that the neighbour's amplifier is too loud
Call # 503	permit fee refund request
Call # 504	hookah pipe smoking vs. tobacco smoking by-law
Call # 507	neighbour's BBQ smoke gets in to her apartment unit
Call # 508	sewage disposal; system application inquiry
Call # 509	mice problem & pest control inquiry
Call # 512	sewage disposal system application inquiry
Cal # 513,	water damage in the apartment
Call #516	suspected foodborne illness after eating at a West Vancouver fish market & cafe the day before
Call # 519	proposed nail spa
Call # 520	selling homemade food and health requirement
Call # 522	permit fee refund request

PETER K. P. LEE

Call # 529 hoarding problem of an occupant in a strata condo in West Vancouver

Call # 531 complaint regarding tobacco smoke from downstairs balcony tenant

Call # 537 complaint regarding tobacco smoke outside patio of a coffee shop

Call # 540 temporary food booth permit application

Call # 541 pool flow-meter inquiry

Call # 542 pharaoh ant and old carpet in apartment

Call # 543 tobacco smoke by-law inquiry

Call # 544 inquiry regarding ant problem

Call # 545 complaint regarding smoke coming from neighbour

Call # 546 sewage back-up and disinfecting information and procedures

Call # 547 complaint regarding a neighbour cutting down a tree

Call # 549 Chinese BBQ pork survey

Call # 553 a hotel in North Vancouver cooking food without proper cooking facilities

Call # 558 complaint regarding tobacco smoke from the outside patio seating

Call # 562 suspected foodborne illness incident reported previously found to be caused by a bladder infection instead

Call # 563   trans fat regulation inquiry

Call # 567   commercial warehouse infested with rodents

Cal # 569,   complaint of smoking from next door

Cal # 571,   temporary food booth application request

Call # 572   inquiry of a dead crow outside and West Nile disease

Call # 576   observed food staff wearing the same glove handling different food

Call # 577   suspected food borne illness from a tourist after eating at a Thai restaurant

Call # 585   Foodsafe exam invigilating request

Call # 586   call from fire department and inspection request prior to re-opening after the fire extinguisher discharged in a restaurant kitchen

Call # 588   proposed U-brew operation

Cal # 591,   mould problem in apartment

Call # 594   mould problem in a rental house

Call # 595   Foodsafe instructor application request

Call # 596   Foodsafe certificate replacement request

Call # 598   complaint regarding rail noise complaint

Cal # 599,   proposed make-up operation and health requirement

     PETER K. P. LEE

Call # 603   complaint regarding the Brazilian waxing treatment at a personal service. The wax was too hot and caused burning.

Call # 612   complaint regarding a mechanical noise from the neighbour causing problems

Call # 616   complaint regarding the daycare neighbour making too much noise

Call # 617   inquiry regarding the covering tile requirement for a kitchen

TABLE 1: COMPLAINT / INQUIRY STATISTICAL COMPARISON

Type	Quantity (1986) 12-month period	Quantity (2011) 9-month period
Restaurant / food-related complaint	20	41
Suspect food poisoning	7	13
Pool	9	19
Housing	8	12
Personal services	1	16
Pollution (air / water / sewage)	18	12
Noise complaint	3	7
Vector	13	11
Garbage complaint	12	2
Miscellaneous	19	6
Tobacco smoking	N/A*	17
FoodSafe program	N/A*	48
Trans-fat	N/A*	7
Farmers' market	N/A*	11
Total	**110**	**222**
* - Category was not available in 1986		

Category	Description
Restaurant / food-related complaint	Food stores and restaurants
Suspect food poisoning	Any foodborne illness
Pool	Swimming, whirl, and wading pools
Housing	Private dwellings and apartment complexes
Personal services	Beauty parlors, hair salons, barbershops, massage parlors, etc.
Pollution	Air, water, and sewage
Noise complaint	Party noise, railway noise, traffic noise, amplified music
Vector	Pest control, including rodents, insects, animals, etc.
Garbage complaint	Commercial and private premises
Miscellaneous	Referral/consultation with other agencies, toxic chemicals, etc.
Tobacco smoking	Information about tobacco smoking bylaw (municipal/provincial)
FoodSafe program	Information regarding general program information, certificates, instructor certification, etc.
Trans-fat	Regulation information
Farmers' market	Includes temporary food booth applications, night markets, etc.

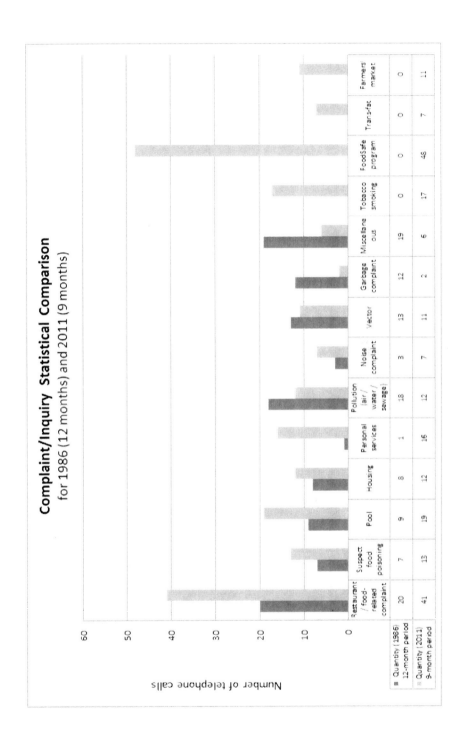

Complaint/Inquiry Statistical Comparison
for 1986 (12 months) and 2011 (9 months)

	Restaurant / food-related complaint	Suspect food poisoning	Pool	Housing	Personal services	Pollution (air / water / sewage)	Noise complaint	Vector	Garbage complaint	Miscellane ous	Tobacco smoking	FoodSafe program	Transfat	Farmers market
Quantity (1986) 12-month period	20	7	9	8	1	18	3	13	12	19	0	0	0	0
Quantity (2011) 9-month period	41	13	19	12	16	12	7	11	2	6	17	48	7	11

Number of telephone calls

Chapter 25

Conclusion

I am very thankful to have a career that lasted almost forty years without too many drastic changes. During this time, I went through only two employers. The last employer was basically the same organization, but changed names four times.

At the time of this writing, many jobs, especially in the public sector with the government, have become privatized. Private sector employment is becoming more and more contractual. Many young employees can only plan for employment that will last a few years. Smart employees are constantly checking and searching for better or upward employment. Also, many private companies and government offices constantly hire new staff and promotions are often from outside sources. Most of the time, loyalty is not valued by the employee and employer. My generation was brought up with the concept that you should be loyal to your employer and not jump from job to job.

During my day, when applying for a job, if your resume showed a frequent change of employers, it indicated that you are disloyal and you likely would not get the job that you are applying for. This attitude changed during the 2000s. If your resume showed frequent change of employers, it indicated that you are a good candidate to hire with a variety of experience, even if the experience was short, like less than a year. Anyways, I enjoyed my long career as a public health inspector. If I had to do it over again, I would still choose the same career. I enjoyed working with the public, even though a small percentage of people were difficult to deal.

I believe that the public health inspector profession will always be required to ensure public safety standards are being checked to conformity. I also believe that there likely will be more changes for PHIs in the future. In fact, at the time of my retirement, the title "Public Health Inspector" was disappearing altogether and becoming "Environmental Health Officer". The newer inspectors were very much sold on the new title. I guess "Officer" sounds a lot better than "Inspector". In the last five years of my career, user fees were very prevalent mainly regarding permit fee and application fee. Perhaps sometime in the future, food premises operators, swimming pool operators, and child-care facilities operators will be billed per routine inspection, follow-up inspection, and complaint investigation. I personally like this billing per inspection system, which would reduce the number of re-inspection because the operators will take extra effort to rectify the violation quickly and fully to minimize additional inspection fees. It could also bring in extra funding for the health department.

I believe that PHIs and EHOs could be privatized eventually and become individual consultants. The government will always look for different ways to decrease the operating budget. I think that these positions will eventually be eliminated in the name of cutting budgets. The food premises operators, swimming pool operators, and child-care facility operators will have to obtain a satisfactory inspection report at least annually from a certified PHI or EHO to maintain a valid operating permit. Of course, the operators will have to pay the necessary fee for obtaining such an inspection report. If privatization takes place, a private regulatory body or association will be required to ensure uniformity in health standards is being kept up and not being jeopardised.

As for myself, I will continue to teach the Foodsafe and Marketsafe courses which will give me a chance to connect with the public and also assisting them to obtain the knowledge to be an operator of restaurants and farmers markets. It is a joy to give back to society by offering to teach Foodsafe courses free of charge from time to time to non-profit charitable organizations.

Teaching keeps me in touch with my former colleagues at the health department which allows me to maintain the friendships and network with them. Sometimes I miss my former working place. I remember having many laughs and many good times.

Of course I will continue the regular coffee meetings with Steve and Sally, both who are former health inspectors whom I had worked with. We have kept up these regular coffee meetings for a long time even way before my retirement. We always enjoy the conversation and occasional sharing of the old days.

It also remains a pleasant surprise when, unexpectedly, on multiple occasions, a person would greet me by name in a store, a restaurant, or a parking lot as I do my daily errands and when I look up, I'd recognize them as a former operator in my district that I had worked with, or it would be one of my many former students. The contact with the public continues on amicably even after my retirement.

Finally, after almost three years of sporadic working on this memoir, I have come to the end of a project that I thought would never end. During this process, when I was discouraged and wanted to give up many times, it was my family who encouraged and reminded me with suggestions to assist me to achieve this goal.

Chapter 26

Photographs

Sturgeon Health Unit, Redwater, Alberta (located in the new
Redwater Hospital) Brand New one man sub office in 1973. This
was where I started my career as a Public Health Inspector.

Inside the brand new one-man office in Redwater in
1973. I had this small but new office all to myself.

1973, walking from my office to my car parked
outside the Redwater Hospital.

PETER K. P. LEE

1973, on an Alberta dirt and dusty country road with my Health Unit car.

1972, doing my 3 months' PHI practicum during
Inspection of a new subdivision application in Prince
George, with the BC Government health unit car.

1973, collecting a water sample from the village of Newbrook, Alberta

1973, inspecting a landfill in Egremont, Alberta.

PETER K. P. LEE

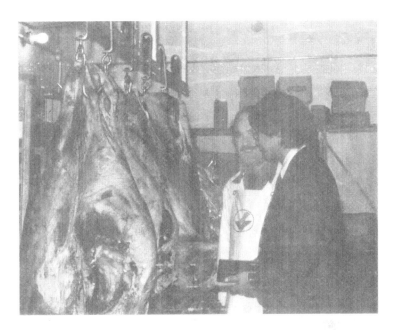

1976? Inspecting a butcher shop and talking to a
butcher on Lonsdale, North Vancouver.

1976? Inspecting a Sears' restaurant in North
Vancouver, Capilano Mall. Jacket and tie attire

2003, Office in West Vancouver Community Centre

1988, North Vancouver Office on Esplanade facing Lonsdale Quay

PETER K. P. LEE

2008, Health Protection Cap & Vest

1985, North Vancouver Office

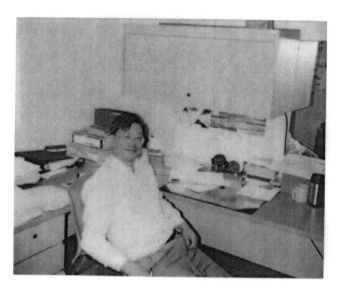

2000, West Vancouver Office which was converted from a senior home.

PETER K. P. LEE

2006, Wearing the Health Department uniform,
Hat and Jacket (front and back).

2005, my wife admiring the flowers outside the Redwater Health Centre.

2005, standing outside the Redwater Health Centre.

PETER K. P. LEE

1981, CUPE 389 striking headquarters, North Vancouver. Me sitting at the far left. This municipal strike lasted about three months in the metro Vancouver area from February to the end of April.

"1973-1975, the fourplex apartment that I was living in Redwater, Alberta"